MY SERVANT BRIGHAM

Portrait of a Prophet

Brigham Young

MY SERVANT BRIGHAM

Portrait of a Prophet

Richard Neitzel Holzapfel
& R. Q. Shupe

BOOKCRAFT
Salt Lake City, Utah

Library of Congress Catalog Card Number: 97-77837
ISBN 1-57008-351-7

First Printing, 1997

Printed in the United States of America

For

Jeni Broberg Holzapfel
and
Susan Taylor Shupe

I give unto you *my servant Brigham* Young to be president over the Twelve traveling council; which Twelve hold the keys to open up the authority of my kingdom upon the four corners of the earth, and after that to send my word to every creature. (Revelation given to Joseph Smith the Prophet, at Nauvoo, Illinois, 19 January 1841.)

Dear and well-beloved brother, Brigham Young, verily thus saith the Lord unto you: *My servant Brigham,* it is no more required at your hand to leave your family as in times past, for your offering is acceptable to me. I have seen your labor and toil in journeyings for my name. I therefore command you to send my word abroad, and take especial care of your family from this time, henceforth and forever. Amen. (Revelation given through Joseph Smith the Prophet, in the house of Brigham Young, at Nauvoo, Illinois, 9 July 1841.)

CONTENTS

ACKNOWLEDGMENTS

We appreciate the encouragement and the efforts of many individuals in helping to bring this project to its conclusion. These include Wendy Agle; Leonard J. Arrington; Aimee Boglietto; Joseph Bauman; Davis Bitton; Gregory Christofferson; Truman Clawson; Lindsey S. Curtis; Stephen Edmunds; Mary E. V. Hill; Jeni, Nathan, and Zachary Holzapfel; Winifred Cannon Jardine; Karna Jones; Matthew Moore; Kirsten Reid; Stephen Smoot; Gene and Deila Taylor; Nelson Wadsworth; and Elden J. Watson.

We also want to thank Cory Maxwell, Jana Erickson, and George Bickerstaff of Bookcraft; and the following individuals from the Church Archives, the Church Library, the Museum of Church History and Art, and the Visual Resource Library, The Church of Jesus Christ of Latter-day Saints, Salt Lake City: Ronald O. Barney, Randall Dixon, Melvin L. Bashore, Dale Beecher, Gaylen Chapman, Chris Cox, Robert Davis, Linda Haslam, Glen Leonard, Veneese Nelson, Bruce Pearson, Merri Platt, Brian Reeves, Larry R. Skidmore, William Slaughter, Steven R. Sorensen, Ronald Watt, and April Williamson.

Many other individuals, representing various organizations and institutions, kindly and professionally assisted us. These include Curt Bench, Benchmark Books, Salt Lake City; Chris Hodges, Charlotte Stewart, and Kim Thompson, Borge B. Anderson & Associates, Salt Lake City; Rick Grunder, Rick Grunder Books, Syracuse, New York; Margaret Adams, Beehive House, LDS Church, Salt Lake City; Geri Tiedeman, Lion House, LDS Church, Salt Lake City; Richard L. Anderson, Alex Baugh, Susan Easton Black, Gary Bunker, Donald Q. Cannon, Richard O. Cowan, Scott Duvall, Lawrence Flake, Linda Godfrey, David W. Hawkinson, Dean Jessee, E. Dale Lebaron, Larry Porter, Thomas Wells, Dennis Wright, and Raymond Wright, Brigham Young University, Provo, Utah; Jeffery Johnson, Utah State Archives, Salt Lake City; Susan Wetstone, Information Center, Utah State Historical Society, Salt Lake City; Lorraine Crouse, J. Willard Marriott Library, University of Utah, Salt Lake City; Peter Schmid, Special Collections, Utah State University, Logan, Utah; Jennifer A. Watts, Huntington Library, San Marino, California; Jennifer Brathoude, Library of Congress, Washington, D.C.; John McMahon, National Portrait Gallery, Smithsonian Institute, Washington, D.C.; Sandra Hildebrand and Tiffany Malone, Thomas Gilcrease Institute, Tulsa, Oklahoma.

INTRODUCTION

A note in the handwriting of Thomas Bullock found in volume A-1 of the "Manuscript History of the Church" records something Joseph Smith said about Brigham Young shortly after their first meeting in 1832:

"About the 8th of November I received a visit from Elders Joseph Young, Brigham Young, and Heber C. Kimball from Mendon, Munroe [Monroe] County, New York. They spent four or five days at Kirtland [Ohio], during which we had many interesting moments. At one of our interviews, Brother Brigham Young, and John P. Greene spoke in Tongues, which was the first time I had heard this gift among the brethren, and others also spoke, and I received the gift myself. Brother Joseph Young is a great man, but Brigham is a greater, and the time will come when he will preside over the whole Church."[1]

Apparently during Brigham's same visit to Kirtland and just after their first meeting, Joseph Smith was chopping wood with Levi Hancock. Brother Hancock later reported that as Brigham approached the two men, and before Brigham was within hearing, the Prophet turned to Levi and said: "There is the greatest man that ever lived to teach redem[p]tion to the world and will yet lead this People."[2] Few, including Brigham himself, could have imagined his future role in the kingdom at this early period and what lay before the Church and the Young family.

Brigham's life has been reviewed by many authors and historians, some more helpful than others. These portraits range from depicting him as a dictatorial tyrant to a non-polygamist western colonizer, contributing to an unfair stereotype. Since the 1970s, major positive steps have been made toward capturing the totality of Brigham's personality. Two of the best book-length efforts are Eugene England's excellent introductory biography, *Brother Brigham*, in 1980, and Leonard J. Arrington's comprehensive and now standard biography *Brigham Young: American Moses*, published five years later.[3] Other historians have contributed insightful details of his life and labors since the publication of these two books, thus adding to our appreciation of Brigham's legacy.[4]

During Brigham's long life he devoted himself to numerous enterprises. In addition both his personal and his public papers contain an impressive amount of documents. While it is difficult to adequately capture any person's life in its fulness and complexity—let alone someone like Brigham, whose life is so well documented—little details can open huge windows into Brigham's heart and mind, thus providing us with the opportunity to move beyond the stereotype. For example, in 1854 Brigham asked the local Salt Lake City bishops to provide a "swing in each ward for the benefit of the children."[5] Because of his concern for the children's safety, Brigham asked the bishops to not allow anyone to use the swing after dark.[6] In 1858 the Historian's Office clerk noted: "September 28, Prest. Young went into his garden and looked at the Comet. . . . September 30, Evening called upon the President, he was in the back yard, observing the 'Comet' through a Telescope."[7] Several months later the clerk observed: "Prest. Young was reading the life of Napolean 1st. most of the evening. He retired about 1. a.m."[8]

Above: BRIGHAM YOUNG ARTIFACTS. FROM TOP RIGHT: YOUNG FAMILY PHOTO-GRAPH ALBUM AND *CARTE DE VISITE* OF YOUNG FAMILY MEMBERS AND CHURCH LEADERS, MONOGRAMMED GOLD CUFF LINKS, JEWELLED SHIRT STUD, GREEN SUN GOGGLES, FRAMED LOCK OF HAIR, AND LEATHER WALLET. COURTESY MUSEUM OF CHURCH HISTORY AND ART, SALT LAKE CITY.

The purpose of this book is not to supplant the important scholarly literature on Brigham's life and world, but from the rich sources available today to provide some lesser-known word pictures and visual images, photographs and artifacts. Of course, we are including here some of the classic stories, quotes, and images, but the heart of this book is the images, many of which have never been published before and were known only to historians, archivists, and curators. The endnotes will lead the reader to the rich and important historical

work on Brigham for a more detailed and useful analysis of his
life and ministry.

As to the organization of the book, part 1 is thematic in ap-
proach, covering such aspects of Brigham Young's world as his
public image, his leadership style, and his personality. Part 2 is a
chronological presentation of the important events and accomplishments of his life. Throughout, the attempt has been to
give the reader, through text and images, a better feeling for
what Brigham's life and world were like.

Each day I (Richard Holzapfel) leave my office on the second floor of the Joseph Smith Building on the Brigham Young
University campus and walk down a hallway that makes a jog
around an atrium before continuing on to an elevator, or further along to the north stairwell in the building. Hanging on
the wall at the jog is a full-size painting of Brigham Young created by his grandson, John W. Clawson. Brigham stands near a
table with his left hand holding a book on the table, his right
arm to a square with the hand holding his coat. He gazes beyond the canvas with deep blue eyes that contrast with the
graying beard. Depicting him during his last years, when Clawson knew him best, Brigham's image grows larger and larger as
one approaches the wall before making the turn at the atrium.

My regular walk down the hall is symbolic of the experience
I had as I began to examine the sources in the various important archive collections about Brigham's life and world. As with
the painting on the wall, the more closely one begins to examine the sources the larger Brigham looms over you. It is hard to
fathom the depth and breadth of his work and life. Sometimes
research left me exhausted as I made my way through the mas-
sive collection of letters, minutes, telegrams, records, journals,
and reports. At other times the experience of spending the day
in the archives left me feeling jubilant as I found something that
gave me a new perspective or insight about him and his world.

Hours of reading and research turned into days, days turned into weeks, weeks into months, and months into years. Now this journey, with numerous stops along the way, has reached another milestone, and what I have discovered to this point is best expressed in a comment by Moses Thatcher. He honored Brigham for his many achievements and then made this observation: "Brigham Young was human and no doubt had human imperfections. . . . The sun has spots. . . . I am not able to bear more light and heat than comes from the king of day with all the spots that obscure his face! I have seen Brigham Young at times when he appeared, much as I can conceive, a greater than mortal man to be. But for my own, and the sake of others I was glad to realize then, and am glad to know now that he was human and doubtless had human frailties."[9]

Brigham, like the sun, had spots. He was the first to admit to human weakness and to the necessity for everyone, including himself, to rely upon the Lord's goodness, mercy, and help. One can choose to dwell on those spots (like the scientist who spends his or her entire professional career on sunspots) or one can enjoy the light and warmth his life and teachings impart. One thing is certain: everything about Brother Brigham was real.

President Gordon B. Hinckley, who has a painting of Brother Brigham hanging in his office, noted his admiration for the man who stood in his place as the President of the Church more than one hundred years ago: "Once in a while I turn around in my chair and look directly back at him [the portrait hanging on the wall] and say, 'President Young, you did a tremendous job. We are trying to do the best we can. Wherever you are, if you can give us a little help, we will appreciate it because we have some very difficult problems.' . . . To me, he stands as a leader whose equal I do not know. He was a man who had great vision, who pondered grand designs, who built nobly and solidly, and who at the same time mingled among the people as their prophet, seer and revelator. Great was his wisdom, tremendous his accomplishments."[10]

NOTES

1. Dean C. Jessee, *The Papers of Joseph Smith,* 2 vols. (Salt Lake City: Deseret Book, 1989), 1:386 n. 2.

2. Charles Lowell Walker Diary, 13 May 1876; see A. Karl Larson and Katharine Miles Larson, eds., *Diary of Charles Lowell Walker,* 2 vols. (Logan: Utah State University Press, 1990), 1:422.

3. Eugene England, *Brother Brigham* (Salt Lake City: Bookcraft, 1980), and Leonard J. Arrington, *Brigham Young: American Moses* (New York: Alfred A. Knopf, 1985).

4. Historians James B. Allen, Davis Bitton, Susan Easton Black, Jill Mulvay Derr, Ronald K. Esplin, William G. Hartley, Richard L. Jensen, Paul H. Peterson, Larry Porter, Ronald Walker, and David Whittaker have each contributed greatly to interpreting Brigham's life and labors in numerous and important articles. Elden J. Watson has collected and published Brigham's manuscript histories and sermons, facilitating an examination of these important sources. In addition, John Welch and John Wm. Maddox have helped place Brigham's discourses into a larger context through their survey of Eugene Campbell's, Hugh Nibley's, and John A. Widtsoe's efforts to collect Brigham Young quotations. Finally, the Church has published a selection of Brigham Young's words in *Teachings of Presidents of the Church: Brigham Young* (1997).

5. Historian's Office Journal, 13 August 1854. Courtesy LDS Church Archives, Salt Lake City (hereafter cited as LDSCA).

6. Ibid.

7. Historian's Office Journal, 28 and 30 September 1858, LDSCA.

8. Historian's Office Journal, 24 March 1859, LDSCA.

9. Moses Thatcher, "Life and Character of Brigham Young," *Contributor* 10 (July 1889): 332.

10. Gordon B. Hinckley, as quoted in R. Scott Lloyd, "'Distinguished Award' Given to Pres. Hinckley," *Church News,* 3 May 1997, p. 6.

Part 1
THE WORLD OF BRIGHAM YOUNG

Chapter 1

PUBLIC IMAGE

An amazing number of people and groups from all over the world (Europe, South America, Asia, and North America) visited Utah during Brigham Young's lifetime.[1] One such visitor frankly admitted, "It is very difficult, if not almost impossible, to speak of the Mormons with feelings perfectly balanced."[2] Prejudice often got in the way of seeing Brigham as he was. Additionally, some visitors spent less than one hour with him and only a day or two in Salt Lake City before making up their minds about him and the Saints. Frequently their impressions were filtered through their own lenses, which often were based upon what they already believed about the claims of the restored Church.

Charles W. Carter, one of the photographers who captured Brigham's image during this period, noted in his "Journal Record of Photographs Taken" an insightful comment about visitors: "Of course, he is the [Lion] of Utah and when in Town all tourists have not considered to have seen all the sights without seeing B.Y. Some parties expect to see all his wives and children, as well—one lady asking to see his wives, in his quiet way, [he] politely informed her that we are not on exhibition."[3]

THE CITY AND VALLEY OF THE GREAT SALT LAKE, UTAH.—FROM PHOTOGRAPHS BY SAVAGE & OTTINGER, SALT LAKE CITY.—[SEE PAGE 513.]

Above: A DOUBLE-PAGE SPREAD FROM THE 16 AUGUST 1866 ISSUE OF AN INCREASINGLY IMPORTANT AMERICAN ILLUSTRATED NEWSPAPER, THE *HARPER'S WEEKLY,* FEATURED THIS ILLUSTRATION OF SALT LAKE CITY AND LDS CHURCH LEADERS. BY 1870 *HARPER'S WEEKLY* HAD A CIRCULATION OF MORE THAN 170,000. COURTESY GARY L. AND CAROL B. BUNKER, OREM, UTAH.

The mail brought news reports and books to Utah, and within a short time it became obvious that Brigham made "good copy." It seems that every month produced some new story, generally fitting the stereotype being created about him and the Church during a period of strong anti-Mormon activity.[4] Even the great mountain walls in Utah could not protect Brigham and his family from constant abuse and from the gaze of the unscrupulous.

Non-Mormon Elizabeth Cumming, wife of the newly appointed territorial governor, noted in a letter to her sister-in-law written after her arrival in Utah in 1858: "We have all been amused with the New York & other papers to-day. The <u>quantity</u> of news about Utah—but amid all the falsehoods, it is

Right: ELIZABETH CUMMING.
COURTESY SPECIAL
COLLECTIONS-MANUSCRIPTS,
MARRIOTT LIBRARY,
UNIVERSITY OF UTAH,
SALT LAKE CITY.

strange that <u>not one single truth</u> should be told—yet such is the fact."[5] One senses from examining the Historian's Office Journal (a daily record kept in the LDS Church Historian's Office located across the street from Brigham Young's home and offices) the apprehension existing in the room as newspapers arrived from the East and were read, only to reveal a situation similar to the one described by Elizabeth Cumming.

Brigham did not generally answer every false charge, vindictive rumor, or obvious distortion. However, when eastern critics raised a cry against him charging him and the Saints with conspiracy in the tragic killing of Captain John W. Gunnison and some of his men near the Sevier River by a local native Indian band, he wrote the secretary of war, Jefferson Davis, in September 1855:

"Contrary to my usual custom in regard to the various false Malicious and slanderous reports set in motion against my character by wicked and designing men I consider the one in regard to the Gunison Masacre . . . [as] one calling for a reply and vindication on my part. I am often made aware of the utter uselessness and folly of seeking to vindicate my character from such foul aspersions as are occasionally raised against me, from the simple fact that although the foul aspersions can be bruited far and wide held to the fluttering breeze by every press and rolled as sweet under every tongue yet when the vile slander is fairly refuted and truth appears in the most incontestible manner it is permitted to lie quietly upon the shelf to slumber the sleep of death or if by chance it should get published in some obscure nook or corner of this great republic be most religiously suppressed as tho in fear that the truth should be known and believed. Still in the case under consideration I feel it a duty incumbent upon me for my own satisfaction and that of my friends as well as the relatives of the lamented Gunison who have desired me to furnish all the details and particulars of that unfortunate occurrence."[6]

Englishman John Mortimer Murphy visited the western United States in 1875 and later published his travel narrative in *Rambles in North-Western America*. During his visit to Utah he took the opportunity to meet Brigham in the Lion House. "He greeted me cordially, though in a dignified manner, and when he read my letter of introduction, told me that anything he could do to make my stay pleasant would afford him pleasure. He said that he was always glad to meet strangers who were visiting the country, and was willing to show them any kindness he could, but that in most instances he was repaid in slander and sarcasm."[7]

When Murphy asked him if he thought all people treated him that way, Brigham replied "that nearly all did, especially newspaper writers and bookmakers," making exceptions for British Lords, and adding, "If we had men like that come here often . . . we should soon be known to the world for what we really are—a sober, chaste, God-fearing people, whose only desire is to be let alone, and to be allowed to worship the Creator according to the dictates of our conscience."[8]

Ironically, when Murphy published the interview in England he added to the stereotype with this critical conclusion: "Thanking him for his kindness, I shook hands and retired, rather prepossessed in his favour; but when I analysed his features mentally, I could apparently see that the suave smile and gloved hand concealed a spirit that would dare and do anything to attain an object once wished for, and that the desire to appear well in the eyes of the world was only for the purpose of gaining converts and confidence."[9]

There was no question about it—news reports, articles, and books discussing Brigham sold. Just months before Brigham's death in 1877, newspaper owner Frank Leslie announced the following to his readership: "The Frank Leslie transcontinental excursion party, whose departure from this city on April 10th was announced in these columns . . . returned safely on June 7th, having in the interval twice traversed the breadth of the Continent. Every place of interest on the route was visited, and its points of significance intelligently studied, and an enduring record made of them by photograph, pencil and pen. . . . The series will be continued regularly until the entire trip from New York to San Francisco and the Yosemite region, including a visit, on the homeward route, to Brigham Young, at Great Salt Lake City, has been illustrated."[10] Brigham equaled the great sites in America as a point of interest.

Few events generated as much interest for visitors, newspaper reporters, and the nation at large than the 1857–58 Utah War and Brigham's arrests and trials in the 1870s.

In the 1850s many federally appointed judges and territorial officers returned East from Utah complaining in the most bitter terms of the LDS Church's influence in the territory. For whatever reason, they were unwilling to accept the fact that the territory, which had been founded by the Mormons, contained an overwhelming Mormon majority and that the economic, political, and social development of the region by the Mormons would reflect Latter-day Saint values. Additionally, many in the nation were shocked in 1852 when Church leaders officially announced the practice of plural marriage.

By the spring of 1857 the nation's capital was abuzz with rumors and allegations charging the Mormons with murder, destruction of legal records, religiously biased courts, and conspiracy with the native American Indians to promote conflict against non-Mormon immigrants. In response U.S. President James Buchanan, without informing Governor Brigham Young, sent a large army to quell a purported Mormon rebellion. When news arrived that the army was on its way, Brigham felt the army was no more than another anti-Mormon mob bent on destroying the Mormon religious community and society.

The earlier experiences of persecution in New York, Missouri, Ohio, and Illinois were still fresh in the memory of many Latter-day Saints in Utah, and the recent murder of Apostle Parley P. Pratt in Arkansas only added to the tension. The muster rolls of the local militia (Nauvoo Legion) swelled from several hundred volunteers to several thousand men.[11] Secretary of War John Floyd, one of many southerners serving in the Buchanan administration, viewed the mission against the Utah Territory as an opportunity to divert national attention from the sectional struggle over slavery.

Citing a history of federal outrages against the Mormon people and the advance of an "armed mercenary mob," Brigham put the territory on full military alert in the early fall of 1857. The Utah War put Brigham on the spot like nothing had before; his words and image appeared dozens of times during the crisis, making Brigham more famous than ever. After a peaceful conclusion to the conflict, the nation's attention turned towards the East on the eve of the Civil War.

Anti-Mormonism now took second place to the larger issues that divided the nation into two separate and distinct societies—

PROCLAMATION

BY THE GOVERNOR.

CITIZENS OF UTAH---

WE are invaded by a hostile force who are evidently assailing us to accomplish our overthrow and destruction.

For the last twenty five years we have trusted officials of the Government, from Constables and Justices to Judges, Governors, and Presidents, only to be scorned, held in derision, insulted and betrayed. Our houses have been plundered and then burned, our fields laid waste, our principal men butchered while under the pledged faith of the government for their safety, and our families driven from their homes to find that shelter in the barren wilderness and that protection among hostile savages which were denied them in the boasted abodes of Christianity and civilization.

The Constitution of our common country guarantees unto us all that we do now or have ever claimed.

If the Constitutional rights which pertain unto us as American citizens were extended to Utah, according to the spirit and meaning thereof, and fairly and impartially administered, it is all that we could ask, all that we have ever asked.

Our opponents have availed themselves of prejudice existing against us because of our religious faith, to send out a formidable host to accomplish our destruction. We have had no privilege, no opportunity of defending ourselves from the false, foul, and unjust aspersions against us before the nation. The Government has not condescended to cause an investigating committee or other person to be sent to inquire into and ascertain the truth, as is customary in such cases.

We know those aspersions to be false, but that avails us nothing. We are condemned unheard and forced to an issue with an armed, mercenary mob, which has been sent against us at the instigation of anonymous letter writers ashamed to father the base slanderous falsehoods which they have given to the public; of corrupt officials who have brought false accusation against us to screen themselves in their own infamy; and of hireling priests and howling editors who prostitute the truth for filthy lucre's sake.

The issue which has been thus forced upon us compels us to resort to the great first law of self preservation and stand in our own defence, a right guaranteed unto us by the genius of the institutions of our country, and upon which the Government is based.

Our duty to ourselves, to our families, requires us not to tamely submit to be driven and slain, without an attempt to preserve ourselves. Our duty to our country, our holy religion, our God, to freedom and liberty, requires that we should not quietly stand still and see those fetters forging around, which are calculated to enslave and bring us in subjection to an unlawful military despotism such as can only emanate [in a country of Constitutional law] from usurpation, tyranny, and oppression.

This is, therefore,

1st:—To forbid, in the name of the People of the United States in the Territory of Utah, all armed forces, of every description, from coming into this Territory under any pretence whatever.

2d:—That all the forces in said Territory hold themselves in readiness to march, at a moment's notice, to repel any and all such threatened invasion.

3d:—Martial law is hereby declared to exist in this Territory, from and after the publication of this Proclamation; and no person shall be allowed to pass or repass into, or through, or from this Territory, without a permit from the proper officer.

{ L. S. }

Given under my hand and seal at Great Salt Lake City, Territory of Utah, this fifth day of August, A. D. eighteen hundred and fifty seven and of the Independence of the United States of America the eighty second.

BRIGHAM YOUNG.

one in the northern states and the other in the southern states. However, once the Civil War was concluded the U.S. Congress looked west again, and by 1871 Utah had become one of the focuses of the nation. The new Grant Administration in Washington, D.C., plagued with criticisms ranging from corruption in the government to problems dealing with Reconstruction in the South, saw the "Mormon problem" as a way to divert attention away from pressing difficulties, just as the Buchanan Administration had done before.

President Grant appointed James B. McKean to take the lead in vigorously fulfilling the Republican pledge to end "plural marriage" in Utah. McKean targeted Brigham for prosecution and with religious zeal moved forward to arrest and punish him by stacking juries with avowed anti-Mormons, accepting virtually any testimony, no matter how dubious, that might bring him to court. On 2 October 1871 U.S. marshals arrested seventy-year-old Brigham and two other Church leaders on charges of "lewd and lascivious cohabitation and adultery." Soon thereafter, McKean secured indictments from a grand jury against Brigham Young and Daniel H. Wells, charging them with murder also. Incidently, some non-Mormons who had opposed Brigham's policies of self-sufficiency earlier in the territory now came to Brigham's support during this time, feeling that the government was using questionable means to accomplish its goal. Brigham was placed under house arrest for 120 days during the ordeal. Eventually the U.S. Supreme Court overruled McKean's methods, nullifying grand jury indictments against Brigham and others.

In one last bizarre courtroom confrontation, McKean presided over what was undoubtedly one of the most publicized divorce proceedings in the United States during this period. In 1873, Ann Eliza Webb Young, a plural wife of Brigham, sued for divorce and demanded a large financial settlement, which Brigham refused to pay. On 11 March 1875 McKean ordered Brigham to pay a $25.00 fine and spend a day in the territorial

prison at Sugar House for contempt when he did not comply with a court order to pay a $500.00 a month alimony while the trial was proceeding. Finally, on payment of $3,600 alimony, the case was dismissed on the ground that, as a plural wife, Ann Eliza could never have been legally married to Brigham.

Brigham himself saw the irony in it all. "One day a man is threatened with fine and imprisonment for entering into what they term an illegal marriage, and the next day it is adjudged that he pay alimony to the woman who the day before, it was claimed, was no wife at all. Consistency is said to be a jewel, but it is certainly a treasure not possessed by the aiders and abettors of the anti-Mormon crusade."[12]

Such inconsistency in how he was treated and viewed by the outside world would continue throughout Brigham's life. And so it was that his public image as portrayed in the popular media of the day usually bore little resemblance to the man whom the Latter-day Saints sustained as a prophet of the Lord.

Upon Brigham's death, George Q. Cannon wrote: "Posterity will yet do him the justice which those who now live have refused him, and in the annals of the Church his Presidency will be pointed to as a remarkable epoch."[13]

NOTES

1. Placing English travel narratives into an interpretative framework is Edwina Jo Snow, "British Travelers View the Saints, 1847–1877," *BYU Studies* 31 (Spring 1991): 61–81.

2. John Todd, *The Sunset Land; or, The Great Pacific Slope* (Boston: Lee and Shepard, 1870), 161.

3. Charles W. Carter, "Journal Record of Photographs Taken," LDS Church Archives, Salt Lake City (hereafter cited as LDSCA).

4. For a detailed and illustrated discussion of the public image of the Church in a broader context, see Gary L. Bunker and Davis Bitton, *The Mormon Graphic Image, 1834–1914* (Salt Lake City: University of Utah Press, 1983).

5. Elizabeth Wells Randall Cumming to Anne Cumming Smith, 9 July 1858, Alfred Cumming Papers, Manuscript Department, William R. Perkins Library, Duke University, Durham, North Carolina; see Ray R. Canning and Beverly Beeton, eds., *The Genteel Gentile: Letters of Elizabeth Cumming, 1857–1858* (Salt Lake City: University of Utah Library, 1977), 85.

6. Brigham Young to Jefferson Davis, 8 September 1855, Brigham Young Papers, LDSCA.

7. J. Mortimer Murphy, *Rambles in North-Western America from the Pacific Ocean to the Rocky Mountains* (London: Chapman and Hall, 1879), 242–43.

8. Ibid., 243.

9. Ibid., 246.

10. *Frank Leslie's Illustrated Newspaper* 44 (30 June 1877): 282.

11. Estimates have ranged from three thousand to five thousand men.

12. Brigham Young to sons Arta D. and Lorenzo D. Young, 21 October 1876; Brigham Young Papers, LDSCA.

13. *Juvenile Instructor* 12 (15 September 1877): 210.

Chapter 2
IN THE LORD'S SERVICE

Ιn his role as a Church officer, Brigham Young was known to be a powerful speaker. There may be more than one thousand reports of talks, sermons, and public addresses of Brigham found in the LDS Church Archives. Of these, many extemporaneous public addresses were published in the *Journal of Discourses,* the *Deseret News,* and the *Millennial Star* during his lifetime.

After taking time to properly edit his spontaneous discourses, Brigham published many of them so that the Saints who were not able to hear him directly would have the opportunity to read his sermons carefully, believing them to be of value. Brigham wrote in 1858: "I would recommend the Journal of Discourses. Bro. George D. Watt has reported my discourses and others and sent them to England and had them printed, which can now be obtained here in volumes. Take them and read them, and if you can, search the volumes of eternity—the volumes of heaven—and see if my teachings do not agree in principle and truth with all the truth of eternity. If they do they are the words of life and salvation to all who will believe, and every man who rejects my words rejects life and salvation to his own soul."[1]

Left: GEORGE D. WATT.
COURTESY RONALD WATT,
SALT LAKE CITY.

Below: OLD TABERNACLE AND BOWERY, CA. 1863. MOST VISITORS AND SAINTS HAD THE OPPORTUNITY TO HEAR BRIGHAM SPEAK IN THE OLD TABERNACLE (AN ADOBE STRUCTURE TO THE LEFT) AND THE BOWERY (TO THE RIGHT) BEFORE THE NEW TABERNACLE WAS COMPLETED IN 1867. COURTESY LDS CHURCH ARCHIVES, SALT LAKE CITY.

Above: "WEST SIDE OF SALT LAKE CITY, FROM ARSENAL HILL," BY CHARLES R. SAVAGE, 3 MAY 1873. COURTESY LDS CHURCH ARCHIVES, SALT LAKE CITY.

Brigham's public speaking career began shortly after his baptism. He recalled: "I was but a child, so far as public speaking and a knowledge of the world was concerned; but the Spirit of the Lord was upon me, and I felt as though my bones would consume within me unless I spoke to the people and told them what I had seen, heard and learned—what I had experienced and rejoiced in; and the first discourse I ever delivered I occupied over an hour."[2]

Brigham's reputation as a speaker among the Saints and the nation at large only increased as his sermons were reported widely. Some listeners and readers were disappointed.[3] Some others were shocked.[4] Recalling something Joseph Smith had taught, he said: "When you speak to a people or person you

Above: "Sacrament in the Mormon Tabernacle" with Brigham preaching, *Harper's Weekly,* 30 September 1871. Courtesy Gary L. and Carol B. Bunker, Orem, Utah.

must use language to represent your ideas, so that they will be remembered. When you wish the people to feel what you say, you have got to use language that they will remember, or else the ideas are lost to them. Consequently, in many instances we use language that we would rather not use."[5]

Recent emigrant Martha Spence [Heywood] noted in her diary in 1850: "Attended meeting and heard the President speak on the principle of receiving the truth in the love of it, his remarks were truly delightful to me and I know that I have always loved the principles he advanced and taught the people."[6] A few weeks later, she recorded, "Last Sabbath of the year of 1850. . . . Regret that I did not attend meeting today as Brigham Young preached."[7]

Two years later another one of Brigham's clerks noted in the official Historian's Office Journal: "Sunday 14 March 1852. Brigham Young rolled out revelation upon revelation."[8]

Even for seasoned Saints, Brigham's sermons often caused

moments of reflection as they recorded their feelings. For example, one member of the Church noted: "Sunday afternoon. President B. Young delivered a discourse, equaled by none that I have ever listened to on 'Space—the Eternities—of matter of duration.'"9 The *Deseret News* adds: "Sunday, Oct. 8, [1854]. . . . An immense congregation were comfortably seated in the open air. . . . While the [sacramental] emblems were being passed, President Brigham Young delivered a highly interesting discourse, which held the vast audience as if it were spellbound."10 Finally, Wilford Woodruff noted in his journal: "Oct. 8th President Young preached to a congregation of several thousand out of Doors And I Believe that He preached the greatest sermon that ever was delivered to the Latter Day Saints since they have been a People."11

In minutes of a family meeting on 25 December 1857, Brigham's long discourse, given at the behest of his sick and homebound sister Fanny, was recorded. At the end of the evening Brigham asked her if the talk was what she wanted: "Sister Fanny, am I not talking to you? Fanny replied, yes, this is my feeling; this day is worth a thousand to me. Let persons be shut up for days and weeks as I am, and they will feel the want of preaching. I read, but I want to hear the scriptures expounded."12

Brigham's power to move people through his sermons is discovered in comments found in hundreds of diaries. For the collective body of the Saints, many situations demonstrate Brigham's ability to rally the people. One such time was in October 1856 when news arrived of the late-starting handcart companies' troubles. After listening to Brigham, Lucy Meserve Smith recalled: "Just at the session of our October Conference, news came where [the] hand cart companies were. President Young and others were so excited and anxious for fear those companies would be caught in the snow in the mountains, they would not go on with Conference. The President called for men, teams, clothing and provisions, and they were soon on

Left: LUCY MESERVE SMITH.
COURTESY SPECIAL
COLLECTIONS-MANUSCRIPTS,
MARRIOTT LIBRARY,
UNIVERSITY OF UTAH,
SALT LAKE CITY.

the way to meet the companies with President Young himself till he got into the Canyon. There he took sick and was obliged to turn back. The sisters stripped off their petticoats, stockings, and everything they could spare, right there in the Tabernacle and piled into the wagons to send to the Saints in the mountains. . . . I never took more satisfaction and I might say pleasure in any labor I ever performed in my life, such a unanimity of feeling prevailed. I had only to go into a store and make my wants known; if it was cloth, it was measured off without charge."[13]

The clerk in the Historian's Office across the street from Brigham's home and offices made the following entry in the Office Journal regarding the Saints' response to Brigham's plea at the October 1856 conference to help the handcart pioneers: "During the last 3 days in reply to a call by Prest. Young the following offerings were made. 26688 lbs flour. 31 bushels & 1 peck onions. 12 lbs dried meal. 5 bushels Oats. $8 Cash—54

teams 6 Horses. 4 Wagons 51 Teamsters 106 Quilts & Blan-
kets. 8 Cloaks. 53 Coats. 51 prs Pants 50 vests 134 prs Boots
& Shoes 29 shawls. 57 Dresses. 72 Skirts. 67 hoods 174 prs
Stockings. 72 prs. Stocks 9 pr Mitts. 14 Socks. 1 small Buffalo
Robe 40 Bundles Clothing (kind not specified) 2 overshirts. 2
Chemises 4 Neckties 13 Hats & Caps 3 Boys Suits. 8 prs
Drawers. 15 Jackets 12 Bonnets. 7 Shirts. 4 Handkerchiefs. 1
Rug. 1 Victorine 5 yds Linsey 2 Aprons. 1 pr Gloves—The list
of Clothing is defective as many persons put in clothing & did
not wish their names to appear."[14]

Of course, Brigham understood his limitations. As historian
Paul H. Peterson has noted, after the Reformation (1856–57),
Brigham came to "realize that he could not 'drive a man or
woman to heaven.'"[15] Later, in 1861, Brigham said: "People
are not to be driven, and you can put into a gnat's eye all the
souls of the children of men that are driven into heaven by
preaching hell-fire. . . . Take that intelligent course, and learn
to instruct people until they increase in knowledge and understanding, until their traditions pass away, and they will become
of one heart and mind in the principles of godliness."[16]

During the tense period of the Utah War (1857–58) one
Saint noted his feelings about Brigham's sermons and life after
attending a meeting in Salt Lake City: "September 20, 1857
(Sunday). To day has but been a repetition of previous Sun-
days. Revelation and inspiration upon inspiration & President
Young presents to my comprehension the many attributes of
the Deity and my constant anxiety is to make him <u>my copy</u>."[17]

The Saints were particularly interested in hearing from their
leader after a long absence, as was the case in April 1859: "Pres.
B. Young gladdened our hearts by his appearance and speaking
on the stand causing quite a sensation."[18]

Non-Mormon visitors often took time to evaluate not only
the content of his sermons but also Brigham's delivery. In June
1865 Samuel Bowles "had a week and an extra Sunday in Salt
Lake City, all passed under the most favorable circumstances for

acquiring knowledge of its people, its institutions, and the natural beauties and phenomena of the neighborhood."[19] He briefly described Brigham as "a well-preserved, good-looking man of now near seventy years; stout, smooth-faced, self-controlled; slow and careful of speech; with a light gray eye, cold and uncertain; a thin, short under-lip and chin."[20] He further reflected: "When his eye did sparkle and his lips soften, it was with most cheering, though not warming, effect; it was pleasant but did not melt you."[21] He then took time to describe a talk he heard Brigham Young give in the Tabernacle while on his visit to Salt Lake City: "It was a curious medley of scriptural exposition and exhortation, bold and bare statement, coarse denunciation and vulgar allusion, cheap rant and poor cant. . . . It was a very material interpretation of the statements and truths of Scripture, very illogically and roughly rendered; and calculated only to influence a cheap and vulgar audience."[22]

Hamilton Hill, another visitor, reported in 1871: "Brigham Young's address was evidently given off-hand, but he spoke with a good degree of fluency; his manner was conversational; his gestures were awkward, but they were infrequent; his voice filled the hall, and he was listened to by all with the closest attention."[23]

Apparently, Brigham's "voice filled the hall" often, as a comment regarding a meeting in 1868 noted: "Conference met at 10 a.m. . . . Pres. B. Young delivered a fine preach. No person has ben so well heard in the New Tabernacle as Prest. Young."[24]

Thus one can find comments by a visitor who enjoyed a particular talk and another, like Bowles, who did not. Most recognized that Brigham did not prepare a text, and therefore his sermons were much different from what one expected to hear from the pulpit of a Protestant church. There were a few exceptions to the general rule, however. The Historian's Office Journal notes: "Friday, Oct. 8. The weather was fair and temperate in Salt Lake City, the thermometer registering 73 degrees at noon in the shade. The general conference of the

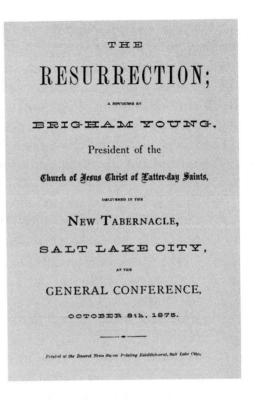

Right: BRIGHAM YOUNG
PAMPHLET, *THE RESURREC-
TION: A DISCOURSE BY
BRIGHAM YOUNG,* DATED
8 OCTOBER 1875. COUR-
TESY R. Q. AND SUSAN
SHUPE, SAN JUAN CAPIS-
TRANO, CALIFORNIA.

Church was continued in Salt Lake City. Prest. Brigham Young
said he had prepared a short discourse on the subject of the resurrection, which he had called upon Elder Geo. Q. Cannon to
read."[25]

And while generally the talks were extemporaneous, Brigham
usually took the time to review and edit them for publication,
as noted earlier. First, he did so because the reporters were not
always able to take down the discourse exactly as it was given.
Second, direct quotes sometimes lost something without the
context, and editing helped Brigham get his message across exactly as he wanted it to come out for an unseen audience. Finally, what Brigham might say in one setting would not neces-
sarily be helpful in a published form. In a few instances a
sermon went to press before he had the opportunity to do this
editing, and this apparently upset him.

His free use of scriptures in his discourses suggests that Brigham had taken the time to study them. Of course, Brigham lived in a biblical environment—the King James Bible was quoted in everyday speech and its stories permeated the air. In his discourses Brigham often quoted and paraphrased the teachings of Joseph Smith. Among his personal papers is a document identified as "Scriptural Quotations." Apparently it is written in his own hand and characterized by his phonetic spelling.

—there is Lords meney and Gods meney but to us there is but one living and true God Elohem Yeho Mikel

—this is life eternal to know the only wise God and Jesus Christ whom he has sent

—the God and Father of our Lord Jesus and the Father of our spirits

—God hath made of one flesh all the inhabetence of the earth

—can eney person officiate in eney of ordenence or laws pertaining to the eternal kingdoms of God with [out] first pasing through them him self [26]

Brigham's gospel knowledge and his ability to stir the Saints with his inspiration, revelation, and vision of the profound gospel message are evident throughout his entire ministry. Church members saw him as their prophet, called to lead them in their efforts to build the kingdom and to prepare for what lay beyond this life.

Brigham's leadership style may best be understood by placing him in the role of a father who loves his family but is often required to teach, instruct, and correct. Certainly, Brigham felt responsibility for the Saints at various times and in different circumstances. However, it was upon his return from the East following the Martyrdom that one can see the relationship develop between himself as the father figure and the Saints as children: "The Brethren ware over joyed to see us come home, for they ware littel children without a Father, and they felt so you may be sure. All things are now reviving up agan. The Brethren prayed with all faith for us to return. . . . I have ben in Councel all most all the time sence I arived here."[27]

Later, while the Saints were gathered at Winter Quarters on the Missouri River in February 1847, he reflected again: "I feel like a father with a great family of children around me, in a winter storm, and I am looking with calmness, confidence and patience, for the clouds to break and the sun to shine, so that I can run out and plant and sow and gather in the corn and wheat and say, Children, come home, winter is approaching again. . . . I am ready to kill the fatted calf and make a joyful feast to all who will come and partake."[28]

On another occasion he said, "Although I may get up here and cuff them about, chastising them for their forgetfulness, their weaknesses and follies, yet I have not seen a moment when they did not love me. The reason is, because I love them so well."[29] A month later, he stated, "Though I may sometimes chastise my brethren, and speak to them in the language of reproof, there is not a father who feels more tenderly towards his offspring, and loves them better than I love this people."[30]

Because he loved them dearly, he noted: "As to the opinion of men concerning myself as a man I care no more about it than I do the dust under my feet. I don't care what you say about me if you will only serve the Lord our God."[31] Having attended a meeting in Salt Lake City, Charles L. Walker noted in his diary: "I felt glad to be there and for the first time in my life after being in the valley over 5 years I had the pleasue [of] shaking hands with Bro Brigham."[32]

Some ten years later, upon the completion of the transcontinental railroad in 1869, Brigham called some two hundred missionaries east during the 1869–70 winter, utilizing the new railway system that linked Utah with the nation.

Elder Thomas Higgs, one of the missionaries called east, wrote President Young from New York with a not uncommon greeting for the Church President that gives us a sense of what many of the Saints felt about Brigham: "Dear Brother and Father, for sutch you have allways been to me. It is with Great pleasure that I address these few lines to you to let you known how and ware I am. . . . [I] arrived in Utica on the eleventh, found my foks all well and glad to see me and I was glad to see them. They received us very kindly. . . . My youngest Bro and Oldist sister I believe will embrace the Gospel. . . . My self and Br Galloway are doing the best we can for the Kingdom of God and it is the Kingdom of God or nothing with your servant and br. In the Gospel of Peace, Ths. Higgs."[33]

Charles Marshall surmised after a visit to Salt Lake City in 1871: "There can be no question that Brigham Young is both revered and beloved by the mass of the people."[34]

In July 1876 a newspaper reporter described Brigham's appearance at the meeting in the New Tabernacle in Salt Lake City: "President Brigham Young addressed the assembled concourse in a kind, fatherly and instructive manner, his words and the feeling that prompted them going direct to the hearts of his hearers. At the conclusion of his brief discourse he blessed the people, every one in his place and station, in the name of Jesus Christ, and by the authority of the priesthood he holds, according to his right and privilege."[35]

Upon Brigham's death, a missionary to the native American Indians, D. B. Huntington, telegraphed Salt Lake asking for a request in behalf of a leader of one of the local Indian bands: "To Whom It May Concern: Fisherman wants to see President Young's remains, so that he can tell his people their father and friend is dead. They will cry hard. He says 'What shall we do? Who will be our friend?'"[36]

How did Brigham engender such feelings among the Saints and those friendly nonmembers in the region, especially in light of the demanding sacrifices he often required of people? Because he himself, by personal experience, knew the "cost of discipleship," he was totally aware of the struggles, privations, and stress that came from gathering, colonizing, and doing the work of building the kingdom. As historian Ronald K. Esplin insightfully observed, "Such shared experience helped create the bond between Brigham Young and his people. At his request and under his direction they gave their all."[37] As Brigham himself said, "I ask not that of my brethren but what I am willing to give myself; and what I do as your leader, or president you should be willing to do the same."[38]

Additionally, Brigham had a knack for putting things in context for the Saints. On 6 October 1859, after the setbacks and disappointments of personal losses, and group losses such as the death of Joseph and Hyrum (1844); the exodus from Nauvoo (1846); suffering and death at Winter Quarters (1846–47); the handcart experiences (1856); the famines (1855–56); and the invasion of Utah by federal troops (1857–58)—after all these difficulties, he said: "We talk about our trials and troubles here in this life: but suppose that you could see yourselves thousands and millions of years after you have proved faithful to your religion during the few short years in this time, and have obtained eternal salvation and a crown of glory in the presence of God; then look back upon your lives here, and see the losses, crosses, and disappointments, the sorrows . . . , you would be constrained to exclaim, 'But what of all that? Those things were but for a moment, and we are now here.'"[39]

Such fatherly wisdom was appreciated and, as the incoming correspondence files and President's Office Journals at the LDS Church Archives demonstrate, was sought for often by thousands of Saints and non-Mormons.

During Brigham's presidency in Utah, he traveled tens of thousands of miles visiting the Saints.[40] It was an opportunity for them to meet Brother Brigham and receive counsel and direction. These visits were important affairs, and the Saints, especially those living beyond Salt Lake City who did not have the opportunity of seeing him as often, celebrated Brigham's arrival.

Hundreds of accounts of these visits survive. One of the most interesting is a report by non-Mormon Elizabeth Kane of a visit to southern Utah just before Christmas 1872. Not only was she an astute observer of life in the Mormon settlements visited but she captured a portrait of the Mormon leader during the visit:

"Brigham Young, 'President of the Church of Jesus Christ of Latter-Day Saints,' makes an annual journey of inspection south, visiting the settlements of his people from the Great Salt Lake to the Arizona border.

"My husband was invited to join his party last winter, and I accompanied him with my two children, boys of eight and ten.

"We left Salt Lake City early one December morning, while the stars were still shining in the frosty dawn. . . .

"I strolled out on the platform afterwards, to find President Young preparing for our journey—as he did every morning afterwards—by a personal inspection of the condition of every wheel, axle, horse and mule, and suit of harness belonging to the party. . . . He wore a great surtout, reaching almost to his feet, of dark-green cloth (Mahomet color?) lined with fur, a fur collar, cap, and pair of sealskin boots with the undyed fur outward. I was amused at his odd appearance; but as he turned to address me, he removed a hideous pair of green goggles, and his keen, blue-gray eyes met mine with their characteristic look of shrewd and cunning insight. I felt no further inclination to laugh. His photographs, accurate enough in other respects, altogether fail to give the expression of his eyes. . . .

"It was the brass band from Parowan come out to meet us, escorted by a troop of many youths. The horses danced and plunged as the band-wagon fell into line, and we entered Parowan in great state to the music of 'John Brown's Body.' . . .

"At these informal audiences, reports, complaints, and petitions were made; and I think I gathered more of the actual working of Mormonism by listening to them than from any other source. They talked away to Brigham Young about every conceivable matter, from the fluxing of an ore to the advantages of a Navajo bit, and expected him to remember every child in every cotter's family. And he really seemed to do so, and to be at home, and be rightfully deemed infallible on every subject. . . . I noticed that he never seemed uninterested, but gave an unforced attention to the person addressing him, which suggested a mind free from care. . . .

"The saints who are more used to his presence take Brother Brigham's arrival at a village tranquilly, but new-comers in Utah greet him much more deferentially than if he were the President of the United States. There was a bright-eyed woman at Parowan with snow-white hair who tried to kiss his hand, and went round to all the party shaking hands with both hands and patting us. She had only been in Utah three months. . . .

Above: "Brigham Young on His Travels," 1873 illustration from
T. H. B. Stenhouse's *Rocky Mountain Saints.*

"There were also plain farmers who had come to seek counsel of 'Brother Brigham,' whether to sell their farms to speculators, or to go shares with them in seeking minerals."[41]

Even upon his return to Salt Lake City, Brigham's traveling party was often met by supporting Saints to welcome him home: "Tuesday [January] 28 [1851] About 10 a m. Gen Wells, Staff & Band go out to meet [Brigham] & escort him to Town. They went out with a large escort about 13 miles north, met the Governor [Young] at Judson Stoddard's when they immediately returned. Arrived in the City at Sundown. The band playing nearly all the way. The cannon roaring until he arrived opposite the State House. On ascending to the Governor's house Mr. Kinkead let fly a number of Sky Rockets [and] Fire Wheels [and] set the air in motion with fire balls. Prest. Young blest the people & thanked them for their kind attentions. His reception was of the heart & not lip service & was truly good."[42]

As a servant in the Lord's kingdom Brigham was either involved in or supervised many significant developments in the Church. He participated in the building and dedication of both the Kirtland and the Nauvoo Temples, and the laying of the

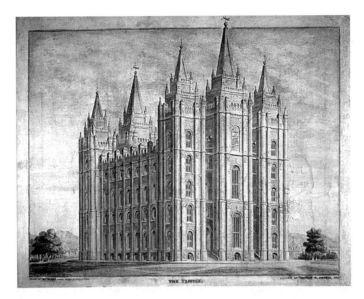

Above: SALT LAKE TEMPLE ARCHITECTURAL RENDERING, 1855, BY WILLIAM W. WARD FROM A DESIGN BY TRUMAN O. ANGELL, WHICH HUNG IN PRESIDENT BRIGHAM YOUNG'S OFFICE FOR OVER TWENTY YEARS. COURTESY MUSEUM OF CHURCH HISTORY AND ART, SALT LAKE CITY.

cornerstones for the temple at Far West, Missouri. Within a few days after his arrival in the Great Basin in 1847 he identified the site of the Salt Lake Temple. While not completed during his lifetime, the temple in Salt Lake was one of his great architectural legacies.

Before his death in August 1877, Brigham oversaw the construction and dedication of the St. George Temple and identified sites for temples at Logan and Manti. Brigham also foresaw the completion of other temples throughout the world,[43] and, in particular, one in Provo, Utah, as the following account explains: "We were among those present and President Young addressing us said, 'We have ascended to the summit of this beautiful hill and now you are standing on Holy ground, the day will come when a magnificent Temple will be erected here to our God and I want you to look and behold the

Holiness to the Lord.

TO ALL PERSONS TO WHOM THIS LETTER SHALL COME:

This Certifies That the bearer, Elder

William L. Binder is in full faith and fellowship with the **Church of Jesus Christ of Latter-day Saints**, and by the General Authorities of said Church has been duly appointed to a Mission to _the British Isles_ to **Preach the Gospel**, and administer in all the ordinances thereof pertaining to his office.

And we invite all men to give heed to his Teachings and Counsels as a man of GOD, sent to open to them the door of Life and Salvation—and assist him in his travels, in whatsoever things he may need.

And we pray GOD, THE ETERNAL FATHER, to bless Elder _Binder_ and all who receive him, and minister to his comfort, with the blessings of heaven and earth, for time and for all eternity, in the name of JESUS CHRIST: Amen.

SIGNED AT SALT LAKE CITY, TERRITORY OF UTAH.

December 7th, 1874, in behalf of said Church.

Brigham Young
Geo A Smith
Daniel H Wells

FIRST PRESIDENCY.

News Print.

Above: MISSIONARY CERTIFICATE SIGNED BY FIRST PRESIDENCY, DATED 7 DECEMBER 1874. COURTESY LDS CHURCH ARCHIVES, SALT LAKE CITY.

scenic beauty of this wonderful Valley, with these grand old Mountains of Ephraim to the North and to the East of us, with their rugged Canyons and towering peaks and to the West, we have a wonderful Lake of fresh water adding more beauty, and by building the Temple here on this spot of ground, there is plenty of room away from the edge of the hill for all needed purposes.'"[44]

During his ministry among the Saints, Brigham contributed

to strengthening and organizing priesthood quorums. He called, set apart, and ordained hundreds to offices and missions. Of particular interest is Brigham's calling or ordination of several Apostles: John Taylor (1838); Wilford Woodruff and John E. Page (1839); Willard Richards (1840); Amasa M. Lyman (1842); Ezra Taft Benson, Charles C. Rich, Lorenzo Snow, Erastus Snow, and Franklin D. Richards (1849); Jedediah M. Grant (1854); George Q. Cannon (1860); Brigham Young Jr. (1864); Joseph F. Smith (1866); and Albert Carrington (1870). Of these, four became President of the Church—John Taylor, Wilford Woodruff, Lorenzo Snow, and Joseph F. Smith.

Furthermore, with "death knocking loudly at his door," as historian William G. Hartley puts it, "President Brigham Young labored restlessly in his last five months of life to reorganize the Church's government structures."[45] These events during the last year of his life are some of Brigham's most lasting contributions to the Church.

NOTES

1. "14 November 1858," Brigham Young Papers, LDS Church Archives, Salt Lake City (hereafter cited as LDSCA).

2. *Journal of Discourses* 13:211.

3. Years later, former Mormon Stephen Forsdick recalled his first experience in Salt Lake City in 1853: "On the sixth day of October, that being the semiannual conference of the Church, we as new comers had the chance to see and here some of the big men of the church. We saw and heard Brigham Young and the opinion I formed of him that day, I never had occasion to change. There is no question about it, he was a man of great executive ability, he knew this power and zealously maintained it. He knew that his word was accepted as law unto the people and he was very careful to cause his influence to increase. His talk was always in the positive and to the point and he showed no mercy to those who opposed him. . . . From the time I joined the church, I had thought of Brigham Young as little lower than the Angels and of Salt Lake as next

door to heaven. I suppose that it was only natural that I should be disappointed, when I found Salt Lake far from being like my idea of Heaven and that after all Brigham Young was just a mortal man." Stephen Forsdick Autobiography, LDSCA.

4. See the reactions to Brigham's sermon in September 1860, for example, in *A Few Choice Examples of Mormon Practices and Sermons* (n.p., 1907), 1.

5. *Journal of Discourses* 12:298.

6. Martha Spence [Heywood] Diary, 24 November 1850, Utah State Historical Society; see Juanita Brooks, ed., *Not By Bread Alone: The Journal of Martha Spence Heywood, 1850–56* (Salt Lake City: Utah State Historical Society, 1978), 37–38.

7. Ibid., 29 December 1850.

8. Historian's Office Journal, 14 March 1852, LDSCA.

9. Journal of the Southern Indian Mission, October 1854, LDSCA.

10. *Deseret News,* 12 October 1854.

11. Wilford Woodruff Journal, 8 October 1854; see Scott G. Kenney, ed., *Wilford Woodruff's Journal, 1833–1898,* 9 vols. (Midvale: Signature Books, 1983–85), 4:290.

12. "Instructions," 25 December 1857, Brigham Young Papers, LDSCA.

13. Lucy Meserve Smith Autobiography, LDSCA.

14. Historian's Office Journal, 7 October 1856, LDSCA.

15. Paul H. Peterson, "Brigham Young and the Mormon Reformation," in Susan Easton Black and Larry C. Porter, eds., *Lion of the Lord: Essays on the Life and Service of Brigham Young* (Salt Lake City: Deseret Book Co., 1995), 258.

16. *Journal of Discourses* 9:124.

17. David Candland Diary, 20 September 1857, LSDCA.

18. Ibid., April 1859.

19. Samuel Bowles, *Our New West: Records of Travel between the Mississippi River and the Pacific Ocean* (Hartford, Conn.: Hartford Publishing Company, 1869), 207.

20. Ibid., 235.

21. Ibid., 236.

22. Ibid., 244–45.

23. Hamilton A. Hill, "A Sunday in Great Salt Lake City," *The Penn Monthly* 2 (March 1871): 132.

24. Historian's Office Journal, 8 April 1868, LDSCA.

25. Ibid., 8 October 1875.

26. Brigham Young, "Scriptural Quotations," Brigham Young Papers, LDSCA.

27. Brigham Young to Vilate Young, 11 August 1844, Brigham Young Papers, LDSCA.

28. Brigham Young to Elder Jesse C. Little, 26 February 1847; as reprinted in James R. Clark, ed., *Messages of the First Presidency*, 6 vols. (Salt Lake City: Bookcraft, 1965–75), 1:318.

29. *Journal of Discourses* 1:33.

30. Ibid., 49.

31. Wilford Woodruff Journal, 15 June 1851; see Kenney, ed., *Wilford Woodruff's Journal* 4:36.

32. Charles Lowell Walker Diary, 26 January 1861; see A. Karl Larson and Katharine Miles Larson, eds., *Diary of Charles Lowell Walker*, 2 vols. (Logan: Utah State University Press, 1990), 1:160.

33. Thomas Higgs to Brigham Young, 14 February 1870, Brigham Young Papers, LDSCA.

34. Charles Marshall, "Salt Lake City and the Valley Settlements," *Frasier's Magazine* (July 1871): 107.

35. *Deseret Evening News*, 24 July 1876.

36. D. B. Huntington, 30 August 1877, Brigham Young Papers, LDSCA.

37. Ronald K. Esplin, "Inside Brigham Young: Abrahamic Tests as Preparation for Leadership," *BYU Studies* 20 (Spring 1980): 310.

38. *Millennial Star* 12 (8 April 1850): 276–77.

39. *Journal of Discourses* 7:275.

40. For an overview of and references to longer studies on this aspect of Brigham's ministry, see Ronald K. Esplin, "Brigham Young's Travels in the West," in *Historical Atlas of Mormonism* (New York: Simon & Schuster, 1994), 102–3.

41. Elizabeth Kane, *Twelve Mormon Homes Visited in Succession on a Journey Through Utah to Arizona* (Salt Lake City: Tanner Trust Fund, 1974), 1, 5, 98–99, 101–2.

42. Historian's Office Journal, 28 January 1851, LDSCA.

43. See Richard O. Cowan, "Brigham Young: Builder of Temples," in Susan Easton Black and Larry C. Porter, eds., *Lion of the Lord: Essays on the Life and Service of Brigham Young* (Salt Lake City: Deseret Book Co., 1995), 227–43.

44. Ben H. Bullock Affidavit, 4 August 1952, LDSCA.

45. See William G. Hartley, "The Priesthood Reorganization of 1877: Brigham Young's Last Achievement," *BYU Studies* 20 (Fall 1979): 3–36.

Chapter 3

FAMILY AND PERSONALITY

Brigham Young's family provided him with much of his happiness in life. Less than a year after Joseph Smith visited his home in Nauvoo and told Brigham that he would not be required to leave his family for long periods of time again, Brigham noted in his diary: "This evening I am with my love alone by my fireside for the first time for years. We injoi [enjoy] it and feele [feel] to prase [praise] the Lord."[1]

Later, he wrote to his wife Mary Ann Angell: "I due think the Lord has blest me with one of the best famelyes [families] that eney [any] man ever had on the Earth."[2] His sermons,

*Janny 18th 1842
this Euening I am with
my wife a lone by my fire
side for the first time for
years we injoi't and
feele to prase the Lord*

THE NEW HAMPSHIRE GAZETTE.

$2 a Year, in Advance.   6 Copies $10.   (The Oldest Newspaper in America—Established Oct. 7th, 1756.)   MARSTON & FREEMAN, Publishers.

PRINTED AT DAILY CHRONICLE OFFICE.   PORTSMOUTH, THURSDAY, SEPTEMBER 11, 1873.   VOL. CVII.   No. 47.   PRICE 5 CENTS

BRIGHAM'S WIVES.

[Chicago Tribune.]

It is not a little curious that Mrs. Ann Eliza Webb Young, wife No. 17 of Brigham Young, should have been wholly unknown until her divorce suit brought her to notice. We know of many Mrs. Young, but never heard of Ann Eliza until quite lately. There is or was Mary Ann Angell Young, Lucy Decker Seeley Young, Clara Decker Young, Harriet Cook Young, Lucy Bigelow Young Mrs. Twist Young, Martha Barker Young, Harriet Barney Young, Eliza Burgess Young, Ellen Rockwood Young, Susan Snively Young, Jemima Angell Young, Margaret Pierce Young, Mrs. Hampden Young, Ellen Roxy Snow Young, Zena Huntington Young, Amelia Partridge Young, Augusta Cobb Young, Mrs. Smith Young, Clara Chase Young, Amelia Folsom Young, and one or two others...

Story of a Mutiny.

[The material for the following sketch comes to the writer from a friend, a gentleman of the medical staff, who was present at the time of the mutiny as assistant surgeon of one of the regiments, and it is undoubtedly true. The officer referred to is General William H. Emory...]

Left. THE 11 SEPTEMBER 1873 EDITION OF *THE NEW HAMPSHIRE GAZETTE,* REPORTEDLY THE OLDEST CONTINUOUS NEWSPAPER IN THE UNITED STATES AT THE TIME, FEATURED NEARLY THREE COLUMNS OF INFORMATION ON BRIGHAM YOUNG'S FAMILY. COURTESY OF R. Q. AND SUSAN SHUPE, SAN JUAN CAPISTRANA, CALIFORNIA.

conversations, and letters, compiled over a lifetime, reveal these feelings time and time again.

When William H. Seward, former governor of New York and secretary of state in the Lincoln cabinet, visited Brigham he noted the special feelings Brigham had for his family as the Young children were introduced: "Brigham Young's manner toward his wives is respectful, and toward his children dignified and affectionate. In presenting them severally as they came in groups, with a kind smile for the particular mother, he spoke this way: 'This is our delicate little Lucy,' 'This is our musical daughter,' 'This is our son George, who has a mathematical genius,' and so on."[3]

Throughout his life, Brigham's family was the subject of intense ridicule and malicious gossip. Almost everyone who came to see him was, as Dean Jessee so aptly writes, "motivated by an inordinate obsession or depraved curiosity to know how many wives he had. Even some of the Saints were inquisitive on this point."[4] On occasion Brigham made reference to this fixation: "A great many men and women have an irrepressible curiosity to know how many wives Brigham Young has. I am now going to gratify that curiosity by saying, ladies and gentlemen, I have sixteen wives. If I have any more hereafter it will be my good luck and the blessing of God. 'How many children have you, President Young?' I have forty-nine living children, and I hope to have a great many more. Now put that down. I impart this information to gratify the curiosity of the curious."[5]

In light of such intense interest in his personal life, Brigham's efforts to shield his family from continued degradation is understandable.[6] In the end, fifty-six children, one hundred and forty-six grandchildren, and twenty-two great-grandchildren were born during Brigham's lifetime. By the time of his death

Brigham had married numerous times (some for time and others for eternity).[7] Sixteen women gave birth to Brigham's children. Emmeline Free had ten; six wives had only one child. The oldest child, Elizabeth Young Ellsworth, was fifty-two at Brigham's death, and the youngest, Fannie Young Clayton, was seven. Of the forty-six children he raised to maturity, seventeen were sons and twenty-nine daughters. Eight wives, fourteen children, and twenty-three grandchildren preceded him in death.

Given the social reality of the nineteenth century, Brigham's love and attention for his family were remarkable. His family responded to his attention. On Brigham's seventieth birthday they greeted him at the Lion House and read a special tribute:

"PRESIDENT BRIGHAM YOUNG, BELOVED HUS-BAND, FATHER AND FRIEND: Wishing to carry out to the letter, the programme of this auspicious day, in which a brief address is included, we beg your indulgence for a few moments.

"Realizing our inability to bestow as much honor, and as high a tribute of affectionate respect as the occasion demands, we have adopted the form of a surprise in order to add to the effect, and enhance the pleasures resulting from our efforts to give you an agreeable entertainment in celebrating this, the seventieth anniversary of your birthday.

"It is a subject of mutual congratulation that your eventful life has been prolonged to this period; and no testimonial that we can confer is capable of truthfully representing our appreciation of your worth and goodness. If the world knew you, as we know you, all parts of the inhabited civilized earth would, this day, echo one grand, universal expression, wishing you long life and happiness; and your broad heart, overflowing with love and kindness, would meet a corresponding warm response from the appreciative bosom of humanity.

"No man living has been invested with as many responsibilities involving the interests and welfare of mankind, and no man ever discharged public duties more faithfully; and yet, with all this, your kindness to, and care for the comfort, convenience and well-being of your numerous family, are deservedly prover-bial. But on this subject, silence might be most appropriate, for surely, all the powers of language couched in the most eloquent strains of expression would fall so far short of reality and the deep feelings of our hearts, as to seemingly desecrate the holy altar of gratitude. Words are insufficient; may God help us to fully illustrate the sentiment in our lives.

"Although your life has already numbered the years which have heretofore designated the allotted time of human exis-tence, as we are now living under the New Dispensation, com-prising the prolongation of the life of man, we may, through the blessing of God, anticipate many future years added to your life. In wishing you many returns of the day, we are not prompted entirely by personal and selfish motives, for we real-ize that you are a mighty instrument in the hand of God for the good of Zion, in the establishment of His Kingdom, and the promulgation of truth for the amelioration of the condition of degenerated humanity.

"In the full exercise of all your mental and physical facul-ties, may you live many years and continue to battle with igno-rance and error until the Priesthood of God is triumphant; and may you enjoy the satisfaction of seeing your family emulate your noble example. May you live till the rulers of every nation on earth shall acknowledge the wisdom of God in your admin-istration, seek unto you for counsel, and recognize you as you truly are, *the friend of God and man*.

"May you live till your soul is satisfied.

"*Lion House, June 1st*, 1871."[8]

Brigham's emotional response on this special occasion re-veals the deep bond that had developed between himself and his family:

"To my family, as well as to the friends who have honored me with their presence, it is perhaps due to say, that this cele-bration is truly a 'surprise' to me; and, indeed, I must say it is a most agreeable one.

Above: BRIGHAM YOUNG AND HIS WIVES. COURTESY LDS CHURCH ARCHIVES, SALT LAKE CITY.

"The whole affair has been quite unexpected, not a word has been said to me, nor a hint given by any person in relation to it.

"The kind feeling evinced in the address which has just been read, and which is manifestly participated in by my family and the friends now seated before me, together with the scene presented, is very affecting to me. I am too full of thought and reflection to give expression to my feelings. But I hope to show, in my future life by example, that I merit your good feelings and wishes; and I trust to see my children and family continue to abide by the counsel given them.

"God bless you all, peace be with you."[9]

In one of the many letters written to family members, Brigham's closing salutation reveals his feelings toward them:

Above: PRESIDENT BRIGHAM YOUNG AND HIS SEVENTEEN SONS, BY CHARLES ELLIS JOHNSON. COURTESY LDS CHURCH ARCHIVES, SALT LAKE CITY.

"Believe me, still, Your best friend, and the benefactor of the faithful. Brigham Young."[10]

Love for his family was an undeniable aspect of Brigham's personality. Another observable characteristic was his sharp wit. Sometimes Brigham's reaction to situations reflected a subtle humor, and at other times his reaction demonstrated an overt effort to produce a little laughter for himself and others.

William Van Orsdel visited Salt Lake City in 1875 to attend the Rocky Mountain Conference of the Methodist Church. He and a friend were admiring some of the houses near Brigham's home when they "saw the Mormon leader himself pacing the walk. . . . The spirit of adventure prompted them and they dared each other to cross the street, speak to, and shake hands with the August leader of Mormonism. No sooner said than

Above: BRIGHAM YOUNG AND HIS DAUGHTERS. COURTESY LDS CHURCH ARCHIVES, SALT LAKE CITY.

done. In a moment the two men were bowing and introducing themselves as Methodist preachers from the West, and proffering eager hands. Brigham Young looked at them with an amused twinkle in his eyes, and cordially shook hands, saying, 'I certainly am glad to shake hands with you. I was a Methodist once myself!'"[11]

In 1851 Mormon convert Elizabeth Green wrote Brigham asking him to remove her name from the records of the Church because she had become a spiritualist. Brigham's reply in part was: "Madam: I have this day examined the records of baptisms for the remission of sins in the Church of Jesus Christ of Latter Day Saints, and not being able to find the name of 'Elizabeth Green' recorded therein I was saved the necessity of erasing your name therefrom. You may therefor consider that your sins have not been remitted you and you may consequently enjoy the benefits therefrom."[12]

Several versions of the following story exist, but in one account Brigham addressed the Saints in Salt Lake City in July

1850 informing them of Zachary Taylor's death. Taylor had been elected twelfth president of the United States in November 1848, but died suddenly on 9 July 1850 from an attack of cholera. He had been somewhat sympathetic to the Latter-day Saints at first, but eventually became an outspoken critic of them, vowing never to let the Saints have a state or territory of their own.

Brigham arose and reportedly said, "We have just received word that Zachary Taylor is dead and has gone to hell." Some federally appointed officers present on the occasion objected and asked Brigham to apologize during the afternoon meeting. Brigham obliged in that meeting. He again walked to the pulpit, where he said, "We announced this morning that Zachary Taylor was dead and gone to hell—I am sorry!"[13]

The often-published story told by Mark Twain about his visit with Brigham, when Twain was still Samuel Clemens, is one of the best stories revealing this side of Brigham: "The second day, we made the acquaintance of Mr. Street (since deceased) and put on white shirts and went and paid a state visit to the king. He seemed a quiet, kindly, easy-mannered, dignified, self-possessed old gentleman of fifty-five or sixty, and had a gentle craft in his eye that probably belonged there. He was very simply dressed and was just taking off a straw hat as we entered. He talked about Utah, and the Indians, and Nevada, and general American matters and questions, with our secretary and certain government officials who came with us. But he never paid any attention to me, notwithstanding I made several attempts to 'draw him out' on federal politics and his high handed attitude toward Congress. I thought some of the things I said were rather fine. But he merely looked around at me, at distant intervals, somewhat as I have seen a benignant old cat look around to see which kitten was meddling with her tail. By and by I subsided into an indignant silence, and so sat until the end, hot and flushed, and execrating him in my heart for an ignorant savage. But he was calm. His conversation with those gentlemen flowed on as sweetly and peacefully and musically as any summer brook. When the audience was ended and we were retiring from the presence, he put his hand on my head, beamed down on me in an admiring way, and said to my brother: 'Ah—your child, I presume? Boy or girl?'"14

While such humor could be used to put the pretentious in their place, Brigham also used his keen wit to open the minds and hearts of the Saints to their own shortcomings so that they might feel the desire to improve. No doubt, too, the smiles that he brought to their faces helped to lighten burdens and make the people glad to find themselves in the world of Brigham Young.

NOTES

1. Brigham Young Journal, 18 January 1842, Brigham Young Papers, LDS Church Archives, Salt Lake City (hereafter cited as LDSCA).

2. Brigham Young to Mary Ann Angell, 20 April 1847, Brigham Young Papers, LDSCA.

3. Samuel C. Chew, ed., *Fruit Among the Leaves* (New York: Appleton-Century Crofts, 1950), 264; as cited in James B. Allen, *The Man—Brigham Young* (Provo: Brigham Young University Press, 1968), 21.

4. Dean C. Jessee, ed., *Letters of Brigham Young to His Sons* (Salt Lake City: Deseret Book Co., 1974), xxxix.

5. *Journal of Discourses* 13:173.

6. According to one report, even though photographs of Brigham's wives "have been taken, they are forbidden to be sold," and therefore visitors were unable to obtain them. See A. London Parson, *To San Francisco and Back* (London: Society for Promoting Christian Knowledge, 1878), 121.

7. See Jeffery O. Johnson, "Determining and Defining 'Wife,': The Brigham Young Household," *Dialogue* 20 (Fall 1987): 57–70.

8. *Deseret News Weekly,* 14 June 1871.

9. Ibid.

10. Brigham Young to Mrs. Young and Family, 23 May 1857; Brigham Young Papers, LDSCA.

11. Stella W. Brummitt, *Brother Van* (New York: Missionary Education Movement of the United States and Canada, 1919), 65–66.

12. Brigham Young to Elizabeth Green, undated; as cited in Leonard J. Arrington, *Brigham Young: American Moses* (New York: Alfred A. Knopf, 1985), 199.

13. Another version of the story is found in Stanley P. Hirshon, *The Lion of the Lord: A Biography of Brigham Young* (New York: Alfred A. Knopf, 1969), 111.

14. Mark Twain, *Roughing It* (Hartford, Conn.: American Publishing Company, 1872), 112.

Part 2

THE LIFE OF
BRIGHAM YOUNG

Chapter 4
THE EARLY YEARS

Born in Whitingham, Vermont, on 1 June 1801, Brigham was the ninth of eleven children born to John and Abigail (Nabby) Howe Young.[1] As a young boy Brigham moved with his parents to central New York state and then to south-central New York, before his mother died of tuberculosis in 1815, when he was fourteen.

Brigham left home, after only eleven days of formal schooling, and became an apprentice carpenter, painter, and glazier (window and glass maker) in Auburn, New York. Following five years of work in that community he moved to Port Byron, where he continued in his occupation. He married sixteen-year-old Miriam Works on 5 October 1824, and within a year his first child, Elizabeth, was born. Three years later the Young family moved to Oswego, a port on Lake Ontario, and a year later to Mendon, New York. Here Brigham experienced both joy and sorrow. His second child, Vilate, was born in 1830; he and his wife were baptized in 1832; and later, his wife died in September 1832.

At some time during this period Brigham began to keep a small diary, in it reflecting on his baptism and subsequent short

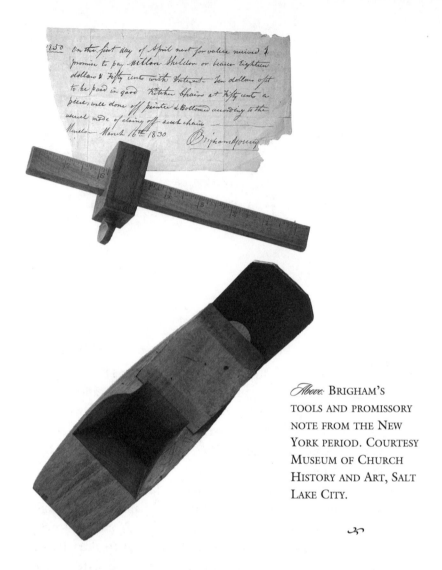

missions. The latter included a visit to Kirtland, where Joseph Smith made the observation regarding Brigham's prophetic calling. The dating of Brigham's baptism is complicated by the fact that he apparently attempted to clarify the date.[2] Elsewhere it had been published as 14 April. Brigham's later correction, however, as already noted, gives the date as 15 April 1832. Yet his earliest diary and a fragment of a membership certificate suggests 9 April 1832 as the date of the baptism.

"Apriel 9th 1832. I was Baptized under the hand of Ebezer

[Eleazer] Miller and ordained, preact [preached] as opertunity prezented Baptized Rachel Flumerfielt. June went to Hector, preacht [preached] at hener <retta> July <6> Baptized John D. Morgan. oct went to Reding from [there] to Hornby, held <Baptized 3> 3 metings then retur<d> to Pattin held 2 metings from their to Reding held 1 meting, from their to Hektor held 1 meting, from their home, from their to Arvon held metin and in the ajacents towns Baptized 4 in Arvon Brother Heber Kimbel [Kimball] and Brother Joseph Young, and my self went to Ohio Baptized Sister Whitney' Father and then returned hom [home] then to woresaw [Warsaw] held several meting."[3]

In January 1833 Brigham went to Canada on a brief mission with his brother Joseph. From July through September he was in the eastern states. By September 1833 he had moved to Kirtland, and on 18 February 1834 Brigham married Mary Ann Angell. Between May and July 1834 he participated in Zion's Camp, which traveled to Missouri under Joseph Smith's leadership. Within a year he was called to be a member of the Quorum of the Twelve Apostles. He helped build the Kirtland Temple, applying his training as a carpenter and glazier. He also acted as superintendent for the painting work on the upper and lower interior courts in February 1836.

Left: KIRTLAND TEMPLE
WINDOW, CA. 1975.
BRIGHAM AND JOSEPH
YOUNG BUILT THE FRAMES
AND INSTALLED AND GLAZED
THE ORIGINAL WINDOWS,
DEMONSTRATING THEIR
HIGH SKILL ON THE CURVED
MULLIONS AND FRAMES OF
THE GOTHIC AND THE
ELLIPTICAL-SHAPED WINDOWS
ON THE EAST AND WEST
FACADES, WHICH WERE
DIFFICULT TO PRODUCE
WITH THE SIMPLE HAND-
PLANES AVAILABLE TO THEM.
BRIGHAM LATER ATTENDED
THE DEDICATION OF THE
BUILDING ON 27 MARCH
1836. COURTESY RLDS
CHURCH ARCHIVES, INDE-
PENDENCE, MISSOURI.

Brigham was busy during the next few months when he went on a summer mission to the eastern states and New England. On 18 December 1836 his wife bore him twins, son Brigham Young Jr. and daughter Mary Ann Young. In March-June 1837 he went on a business mission to the eastern states with Willard Richards, and then between June and August on a mission to New York and Massachusetts. During the fall disaster struck when shock waves caused by a general economic collapse in the United States hit the financial institution the brethren had organized in Kirtland. After its failure, some Latter-day Saints turned against Joseph Smith. Because of Brigham's

TO WHOM IT MAY CONCERN:

THIS Certifies that ~Brigham Young,~ has been received into the church of the Latter Day Saints, organized on the sixth of April, in the year of our Lord, one thousand, eight hundred, and thirty, and has been ordained an elder according to the rules and regulations of said church, and is duly authorized to preach the gospel, agreeably to the authority of that office.

From the satisfactory evidence which we have of his good moral character, and his zeal for the cause of righteousness, and diligent desire to persuade men to forsake evil and embrace truth, we confidently recommend him to all candid and upright people as a worthy member of society.

We, therefore, in the name, and by the authority of this church, grant unto this our worthy brother in the Lord, this letter of commendation as a proof of our fellowship and esteem: praying for his success and prosperity in our Redeemer's cause.

Given by the direction of a conference of the elders of said church, assembled in Kirtland, Geauga county, Ohio, the third day of March, in the year of our Lord one thousand, eight hundred, and thirty six.

Above: BRIGHAM YOUNG'S ELDER'S CERTIFICATE, DATED 30 MARCH 1836. COURTESY LDS CHURCH ARCHIVES, SALT LAKE CITY.

continued support of the Prophet, he was forced to leave Kirtland on 22 December. He made his way to the new gathering site, arriving in Far West, Missouri, on 14 March 1838.

Brigham, like the other Saints, did not stay long in Missouri. Following Joseph Smith's arrest and incarceration in 1838, as senior member of the Quorum of Twelve Brigham directed the evacuation of the Latter-day Saints from Missouri when they were driven from the state during the winter.

By mid-March 1839 Brigham had moved his own family to Quincy, Illinois. Within a few months he returned briefly to Far West to fulfill the revelation received by Joseph Smith on 8 July 1838. That revelation instructed the members of the Quorum of the Twelve Apostles to assemble in Far West, Missouri, on 26 April 1839 and thereafter "depart to go over the great waters, and there promulgate" the gospel (see Doctrine and Covenants 118).

In May, upon his return to Illinois, Brigham moved his family again, this time to Montrose, Iowa, preparing to make the long journey to the British Isles. On 4 September his daughter Alice Young was born, and within a few days he left for his mission to England. In October, Brigham's father died.

Lancashire to wit. } THESE are to certify, that at the General Quarter Sessions of the Peace, held by adjournment at *Preston* in and for the said County, the *eighth* day of *April* in the *third* Year of the Reign of Her Majesty Queen Victoria, *Brigham Young* came before the Justices present, and did then and there in open Court, take the Oaths appointed to be taken in the Stead of the Oaths of Allegiance and Supremacy, and also the Abjuration Oath ; and did also then and there make and repeat the Declaration against Popery ; and also the Declaration required to be taken by Dissenting Ministers, and subscribed his name severally thereto, pursuant to the several Statutes in that behalf made and provided.

Deputy Clerk of the Peace in and for the said County of Lancaster.

Above: BRIGHAM YOUNG'S ENGLISH JUSTICE OF THE PEACE CERTIFICATE, DATED 8 APRIL 1840. COURTESY LDS CHURCH ARCHIVES, SALT LAKE CITY.

On 7 March 1840 Brigham finally left New York for England, landing there on 6 April. On 14 April, Brigham officially succeeded to the presidency of the Quorum of the Twelve.

In twelve short months these stalwart missionaries were instrumental in converting literally thousands to the Church. Brigham left England on 21 April 1841, arriving in Nauvoo on 1 July with Heber C. Kimball and John Taylor.

Within a week after Brigham's arrival home from the successful mission in the British Isles, Joseph Smith visited him and said: "Dear and well-beloved brother, Brigham Young, verily thus saith the Lord unto you: My servant Brigham, it is no more required at your hand to leave your family as in times past, for your offering is acceptable to me. I have seen your labor and toil in journeyings for my name. I therefore command you to send my word abroad, and take especial care of your family from this time, henceforth and forever. Amen."[4]

Brigham took advantage of the opportunity to stay close to the Prophet in Nauvoo. He recalled in 1868: "I never did let an opportunity pass of getting with the Prophet Joseph and of

Right: BRIGHAM
YOUNG, 1841;
COPIED FROM THE
YOUNG WOMAN'S
JOURNAL 8 (JULY
1897): 438. THIS
PAINTING APPAR-
ENTLY REPRESENTS
THE FIRST KNOWN
VISUAL IMAGE OF
BRIGHAM YOUNG.

hearing him speak in public or in private, so that I might draw understanding from the fountain from which he spoke, that I might have it and bring it forth when it was needed. . . . Such moments were more precious to me than all the wealth of the world. No matter how great my poverty . . . I never let an opportunity pass of learning what the Prophet had to impart. This is the secret of the success of your humble servant."[5]

On 4 September he was elected to the Nauvoo City Council, and on 8 November he offered the dedicatory prayer for the baptismal font in the Nauvoo Temple, which was being built at the time.

The year 1842 was an important one for Brigham, for it was then that he received his washings, anointings, and endowments

Above: JOSEPH SMITH'S RED BRICK STORE, CA. 1885. COURTESY LDS CHURCH ARCHIVES, SALT LAKE CITY.

from Joseph Smith on 4 May in Joseph's store on Water Street, known today as the Red Brick Store. He recalled those events at the dedication of the first temple in Utah more than thirty-five years later: "[It was before the Temple was completed and in the upper room over Joseph's Red Brick Store] where we [received] our [endowments] under the hands of the Prophet Joseph in Nauvoo. We had only one room [in which to receive the ordinances], with the exception of a little side room or office. [In this side office] we were washed and anointed, [and] had our garments placed upon us. . . . After he had performed these ceremonies . . . we went into the large room over the store. . . . Joseph [had] divided up the room the best he could. [He] . . . gave us our instructions as we passed along from one department to another. . . . And after we [were] through, Bro[ther] Joseph turned to me and said, 'Bro[ther] Brigham, this is not arranged right. But we have done the best we could under the circumstances in which we are placed. And I wish [for] you to take this matter in hand, and organize and systemize all these ceremonies. . . .' [We performed the ordinances under Joseph's supervision many times] and each time I got something more, so that when we [performed them in] the Temple at Nauvoo, I understood and knew how to place them there. We had our ceremonies pretty correct."[6]

Brigham and the Quorum of the Twelve continued to receive additional assignments and responsibilities from Joseph Smith, and on 18 May he was appointed to serve on a committee to aid immigrants.

During this period Brigham struggled with and finally accepted the revelation on plural marriage. With Mary Ann's consent, Brigham married Lucy Ann Decker Seeley in June 1842, the first of several women brought into his family. Shortly thereafter, Brigham's daughter Elizabeth Young married Edmund Ellsworth. Now Brigham entered a new phase of life as a father-in-law.

In 1843, Brigham as the President of the Twelve began the attempt to bring Oliver Cowdery back to the Church. In a letter dated 19 April 1843, Brigham and members of the Twelve wrote "An epistle of The Twelve, in Council assembled, to Oliver Cowdery, one of the witnesses to the Book of Mormon."[7] Addressing Oliver as "Dear Brother," Brigham and his brethren told Oliver that they "reflected upon the time when we had met together, when we were brethren, when we were one, & took sweet counsel together."[8] They added: "We thought perhaps our old [and] esteemed friend might by this time have felt his lonely solitary situation; might feel that he was a stranger in a strange land, & had wandered long enough from his Fathers house, & that he might have a disposition to return."[9]

They hoped Oliver was ready to return and informed their brother: "If this is the case, all that we have got to say, is, your brethren are ready to receive you, we are not your enemies, but your brethren. Your dwelling place you know ought to be in Zion—Your labor might be needed in Jerusalem, & you ought to be the servant of the living God." In closing, they added: "In the bonds of the New and Everlasting Covenant we remain your unchangeable friends in the Gospel."[10]

In July Brigham entered another phase of life, as his first grandchild was born, granddaughter Charlotte Ellsworth. During July-October he traveled in eastern states to raise money for the temple and for the Nauvoo House.

On 28 December he said: "[N]ever suffer anger to find a seat in your breast, never get angry at all, treat all mildly, govern yourself, your passions, and it will give you power."[11] On 7 March 1844 he was "at the temple all day—the Prophet, Patriarch, B. Young, Taylor &c spoke—both large meetings—a most splendid day—& an attentive congregation—received much instruction—got home about 5."[12]

In an unsigned document, members of the Quorum of the Twelve recounted events of March 1844, just months before the deaths of Joseph and Hyrum Smith. The document begins: "We the undersign, do hereby solemnly, sincerely, and truly testify before God, Angels, and men, unto all people whom this certificate may come, that we were present at a Council in the latter part of the month of March last, held in the city of Nauvoo in the upper part of the brick building situate upon Water Street, commonly known here as 'Joseph's Store,' [known today as the Red Brick Store] in which Council Joseph Smith did preside; and the greater part of the Twelve Apostles were present."[13]

During this meeting, "Joseph Smith seemed somewhat depressed in Spirit, and took the liberty to open his heart to us concerning his presentiments of the future."[14] The document then reports the substance of Joseph's word to those present: "'Brethren, the Lord bids me hasten the work in which we are engaged. . . . It may be that my enemies will kill me, and in case they should, and the keys and power which rest on me not be imparted to you, they will be lost from the Earth; but if I can only succeed in placing them upon your heads, then let me fall a victim to murderous hands if God will suffer it, and I can go with all pleasure and satisfaction, knowing that my work is done, and the foundation laid on which the Kingdom of God is to be reared in this dispensation of the fulness of times. Upon the shoulders of the Twelve must the responsibility of leading

Above: "Joseph Smith and His Friends," by William W. Major, ca. 1845. William Warner Major, a self-trained artist from Bristol, England, converted to Mormonism and emigrated to Nauvoo in 1844. Within a year he began working on several projects, including this one of the Church leaders completed some time after the martyrdom of Joseph and Hyrum Smith. It depicts several members of the First Presidency and of the Quorum of the Twelve Apostles. They are, from left to right, Hyrum Smith, Willard Richards, Joseph Smith, Orson Pratt, Parley P. Pratt, Orson Hyde, Heber C. Kimball, and Brigham Young. Courtesy Museum of Church History and Art, Salt Lake City.

this Church hence forth rest until you shall appoint others to succeed you. . . .' After this appointment was made, and confirmed by the holy anointing under the hands of Joseph and Hyrum, Joseph continued his speech unto them, saying, while he walked the floor and threw back the collar of his coat upon his shoulders, 'I roll the burden and responsibility of leading this Church off from my shoulders on to yours. Now, round up your shoulders and stand under it like men; for the Lord is going to let me rest awhile.'"[15]

NOTES

1. Much of what we know about Brigham comes from his own discourses and diaries and manuscripts. Brigham's early history, based on the "Manuscript History of Brigham Young, and History of Brigham Young, 1801–44," was originally published in the *Deseret News* in 1857 and 1858. Three holograph diaries in Brigham's own handwriting cover the period 1832 through 1844. Other diaries and journals, kept by clerks, cover later years. Finally, clerks worked for years to compile Brigham's history, some 57 volumes of material, which was of course edited material collected from various sources and placed in the first person.

2. *Journal of Discourses* 9:219.

3. Brigham Young Journal, 1832, Brigham Young Papers, LDS Church Archives, Salt Lake City; hereafter cited as LDSCA. (< > indicates material inserted by Brigham Young above the line as he went back to add material to the text.)

4. Doctrine and Covenants 126. First published in the *Deseret News* (18 April 1855), this was included as section 126 in the 1876 and subsequent editions of the Doctrine and Covenants.

5. *Journal of Discourses* 12:269–70.

6. L. John Nuttall Diary, 7 February 1877, Archives and Manuscripts, Harold B. Lee Library, Brigham Young University, Provo, Utah.

7. "An Epistle of The Twelve, in Council assembled, to Oliver Cowdery, one of the witnesses to the Book of Mormon," 19 April 1843, LDSCA.

8. Ibid.

9. Ibid.

10. Ibid.

11. Wilford Woodruff Journal, 28 December 1843; see Scott G. Kenney, ed., *Wilford Woodruff's Journal, 1833–1898,* 9 vols. (Midvale: Signature Books, 1983–85), 2:333.

12. Historian's Office Journal, 7 March 1844, LDSCA.

13. "Declaration of 12 Apostles, March 1844," Brigham Young Papers, LDSCA.

14. Ibid.

15. Ibid.

Chapter 5

THE PROPHET'S MANTLE

Within a few months of the "Last Charge" meeting with the Twelve in March 1844, Brigham went on a short-term mission. While in the East he received word that Joseph and Hyrum had been murdered in Carthage. Later, in an 1849 meeting where several new Apostles were ordained, Brigham revealed what had happened and how he had felt during that critical period of Church history.

"Previous to attending to the ordinations I want to lay certain principles before the Brethren concerning our present situation. In the first place, say here what never said since Joseph's death till now. I was in Bro. Beamants house in Petersborough. They received letters from Nauvoo giving account of mob, death &c. When we got that letter Orson Pratt and I were there and read the letter. I felt then as I never felt in my life. All disappointments, losses, and crosses never bring a tear. Bringing it to mind brings tears. My head felt so distressed I felt as though it would crack. It come to me Joseph and Hyrum are gone, is the Priesthood taken from the Earth. I had forgot myself. The organization of the Kingdom and Church passed before me. It came like a clap. It come to me like Revelation—the

Above: BRIGHAM YOUNG, PROBABLY BY
LUCIAN FOSTER, CA. 1844–1845. COURTESY
LDS CHURCH ARCHIVES, SALT LAKE CITY.

keys of the Kingdom are here and was satisfied it was all right. No man ever loved another man more than I did Joseph. When I came to Nauvoo I knew by visions of the Spirit from Twelve there would be a First Presidency. I knew who would be there as well as now. Joseph told the story himself."[1]

Wilford Woodruff recorded in his journal on 17 July 1844: "Elder B. young arrived in Boston this morning. I walked with him to 57 Temple st and called upon sister Voice. Br. Young took the bed" where he gave vent to his feeling in tears.[2]

While the loss of the Prophet had a profound effect upon Brigham, he seemed always to be able to put things in perspective and move forward even in the midst of crushing obligations. In Utah he once reflected: "I feel like shouting hallelujah, all the time, when I think that I ever knew Joseph Smith, the Prophet whom the Lord ordained, and to whom He gave keys and power to build up the kingdom of God on earth and sustain it. These keys are committed to this people, and we have power to continue the work that Joseph commenced, until everything is prepared for the coming of the Son of Man."[3]

Upon his arrival in Nauvoo in August 1844, Brigham moved to reassure the Saints that the Twelve held the keys and hence they were not leaderless. One observer at the important August meeting recalled: "[Brigham] then went to work as a workman understanding his business. He called for the quorums of Priesthood to be seated together, in order, as much as the circumstances would permit, and then presented the matter under consideration in a manner so plain and convincing that all could readily understand that Joseph's mantle had fallen upon Brigham Young. It was self-evident that the power and influence that had rested upon Brother Joseph in the performance of his official duties, rested upon him. This became at once so satisfactory that he, at that meeting, became the unanimous choice of all present. In other words, the quorum of the Twelve Apostles became as the First Presidency of the Church, Brigham Young being the President of that quorum made him the first representative man, or President of the Church."[4]

In a letter written to his daughter, Vilate, Brigham noted: "This much I can say—the spirit of Joseph is here, though we cannot enjoy his person. Through the great anxiety of the church, there was a conference held last Thursday. The power of the Priesthood was explained and the order thereof, on which the whole church lifted up their voices and hands for the twelve to move forward and organize the church and lead it as Joseph had. This is our indispensable duty. The brethren feel well to think the Lord is still mindful of us as a people."[5]

Among the many aspects of "the work Joseph commenced" was the building of the Nauvoo Temple. One of the decisions that had to be made was whether the Saints should remain in Illinois and finish the temple, or should depart before there was

Below: RESTORED BRIGHAM YOUNG HOME. COURTESY SPECIAL COLLECTIONS-MANUSCRIPTS, J. WILLARD MARRIOTT LIBRARY, UNIVERSITY OF UTAH, SALT LAKE CITY.

more trouble. Brigham was confident that he had the keys, as the President of the Twelve, to find out the Lord's will. "Friday, January 24. Brothers Heber C. Kimball and Newell K. Whitney were at my house. We washed, anointed, and prayed. Had a good time. I inquired of the Lord whether we should stay here and finish the Temple. The answer was we should."[6]

During the next two years Brigham directed the continued missionary work, the gathering of the Saints, and the building of the temple in Nauvoo. Privately, he and the Twelve also prepared for the Saints' departure from the city to a location in the West.

About this time W. W. Phelps, a poet and well-known hymn composer in the Church, published a list of titles he suggested for the members of the Twelve, including one for Brigham: "I know the Twelve, and they know me. Their names are Brigham Young, the lion of the Lord; Heber C. Kimball, the herald of grace; Parley P. Pratt, the archer of paradise; Orson Hyde, the olive branch of Israel; Willard Richards, the keeper of the rolls; John Taylor, the champion of right; William Smith, the patriarchal Jacob staff; Wilford Woodruff, the banner of the gospel;

Left. WILLIAM WINES PHELPS,
CA. 1853. COURTESY LDS
CHURCH ARCHIVES, SALT
LAKE CITY.

George A. Smith, the entablature of truth; Orson Pratt, the gauge of philosophy; John E. Page, the sun dial; and Lyman Wight, the wild ram of the mountain. And they are good men; the best the Lord can find; they do the will of God, and the saints knew it."[7]

Through the fall and winter Brigham was busy preparing for the exodus from Nauvoo and completing the temple. The first meeting in the temple was held during the Church's conference that began on 5 October 1845:

"Meeting opened at five minutes to eleven by President B. Young as a form of dedication prayer. Great joy and gratitude was felt by the Saints to realize this blessing which they had so long looked for. There were five thousand persons seated comfortably. . . .

"Monday, 6th. Our general conference assembled in the temple for the first time; much business was done. The Twelve met in council and for prayer, morning and evening, to our Heavenly Father to stay the wrath of our enemies, and to overthrow all their designs, which He has done thus far, and we thank His holy name. Tuesday, 7th. In the morning the Twelve

Above: Nauvoo Temple, by Thomas Easterly, ca. 1846.
Courtesy Missouri State Historical Society, St. Louis,
Missouri.

met for prayer in the usual place. Conference met in the Temple.
. . . In the afternoon, when the Conference was assembled,
Major Warren came in with his posse of troops and surrounded
our cannon, supposing it was a mob, President Young dismissed
the conference and told the brethren to go home, and let every
man be prepared. . . .

"Wednesday, 8th. President Young spoke. . . . This day was
the close of the conference. All things went off in union, not a
dissenting voice in the congregation, and a perfect union ex-
hibited by the Saints to remove from the country the coming
spring. All these things transpire in answer to the prayers of the
Saints, who meet together constantly after the holy order; and
the glory be to the Father, and to the Son, and to the Holy
Ghost for His blessings upon Israel."[8]

Eventually the temple was close enough to being finished that Brigham began administering the ordinances. Before he left Nauvoo some six thousand individuals had passed through the rooms receiving the blessings of the house of the Lord.

During 1846 Brigham personally directed the movement of thousands of Latter-day Saints to the Missouri River Valley, where he established a temporary Church center at Winter Quarters. Brigham reminded the Saints there that the covenants revealed in the Nauvoo Temple were not just some theological concept to be played out in the world to come. He argued that they had practical application, especially in regard to the poor Saints lagging behind them: "Let the fire of the covenant which you made in the House of the Lord, burn in your hearts, like flame unquenchable till you, by yourselves or delegates . . . [can] rise up with his team and go straightway and bring a load of the poor from Nauvoo . . . [for] this is a day of action and not of argument."[9]

When the Saints decided to leave Nauvoo, the movement became known as the "Exodus to Greatness." Many people then saw parallels between their movement and that of the children of Israel. The crossing of the Mississippi was analogous to the crossing of the Red Sea. The bitterly cold days during which the river was frozen were likened to the "parting of the Red Sea." Additionally, when the poor camp of Saints were able to gather the quails that had landed in their midst, it was seen as a miracle similar to the sending of manna from heaven.

On 14 January 1847 Brigham Young received the "Word and the Will of the Lord."[10] In this revelation the Lord again drew a comparison between the modern Saints and the ancient Israelites: "The Word and Will of the Lord concerning the Camp of Israel in their journeyings to the West."[11] Additionally, the revelation utilized language similar to that in the book of Exodus: "covenant," "commandments," "statutes," and "ordinances."[12] Also, the organization of the camp with "captains of hundreds, captains of fifties, and captains of tens" re-

minded the Saints of the passage in the book of Exodus: "Moreover thou shalt provide out of all the people able men, such as fear God, men of truth, hating covetousness; and place such over them, to be rulers of thousands, and rulers of hundreds, rulers of fifties, and rulers of tens."[13]

Again, the revelation echoed the language of the book of Exodus: "I am the Lord your God, even the God of your fathers, the God of Abraham and of Isaac and of Jacob."[14] And more explicitly the Lord referred to himself as "he who led the children of Israel out of the land of Egypt; and my arm is stretched out in the last days, to save my people Israel."[15] Brigham Young became the "American Moses" who led his people to a "promised land" in the Great Basin.

Only four days after Brigham Young completed the 1847 trek to Salt Lake Valley, he walked to a spot between two creeks, waved his hand, and said, "Here is the [ten] acres for

Left. COPY OF AN ORIGINAL DA-GUERREOTYPE. DATING OF THIS IMAGE IS UNKNOWN. IT MAY HAVE BEEN TAKEN IN NAUVOO BY LUCIAN FOSTER JUST BEFORE BRIGHAM YOUNG LEFT THE "CITY OF JOSEPH" IN FEBRUARY 1846, OR BY MARSENA CANNON IN SALT LAKE CITY SOMETIME AROUND 1850. COURTESY UTAH STATE HISTORICAL SOCIETY, SALT LAKE CITY.

the temple."[16] In April 1853 President Young recalled the visionary experience he had at the site: "I scarcely ever say much about revelations, or visions, but suffice it to say, five years ago last July [1847] I was here, and saw in the Spirit the Temple not ten feet from where we have laid the Chief Corner Stone. I have not inquired what kind of a Temple we should build. Why? Because it was represented before me. I have never looked upon that ground but the vision of it was there. I see it as plainly as if it was in reality before me. Wait until it is done. I will say, however, that it will have six towers."[17]

Creating a sense of holiness in the new promised land, the Saints utilized powerful and emotionally laden symbols—such as the all-seeing eye, crowns, the handclasp of fellowship, and the phrase, "Holiness to the Lord," reminding them of the covenant relationship between themselves and God, reflecting these scripture passages in Exodus and Zechariah:

"And thou shalt make a plate of pure gold, and grave upon it, like the engravings of a signet, HOLINESS TO THE LORD. And thou shalt put it on a blue lace, that it may be upon the mitre; upon the forefront of the mitre it shall be. And it shall be upon Aaron's forehead."[18]

"In that day shall there be upon the bells of the horses HOLINESS UNTO THE LORD; and the pots in the Lord's house shall be like the bowls before the altar. Yea, every pot in Jerusalem and in Judah shall be holiness unto the Lord of hosts."[19]

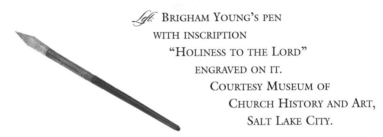

Left. BRIGHAM YOUNG'S PEN WITH INSCRIPTION "HOLINESS TO THE LORD" ENGRAVED ON IT. COURTESY MUSEUM OF CHURCH HISTORY AND ART, SALT LAKE CITY.

Brigham identified the new promised land, but did not stay in the valley very long. Soon he was on his way back to help organize the mass exodus from Winter Quarters. In December he was sustained as President of the Church, and he called Heber C. Kimball and Willard Richards to serve as his counselors in the First Presidency. On 26 May 1848 he left Winter Quarters for the last time and headed to the Salt Lake Valley with some twelve hundred persons following him. Brigham arrived on 20 September. He spoke to the Saints shortly after his return about his feelings of being there with them:

"I trust I shall have strength to speak to be understood. ... I also trust to have command over my feelings to speak in a childlike spirit yet with the confidence and courage of a man although it may be hard to suppress my feelings. . . . I venture [to say] not another person that has the sensations that I have. . . . having to guard every moment [to keep] from bursting

Above: GOLD COINS. BRIGHAM YOUNG, JOHN TAYLOR, AND
JOHN KAY PREPARED THE INSCRIPTIONS FOR THE GOLD COINS
TO BE MINTED FROM THE CALIFORNIA GOLD DUST BROUGHT TO
SALT LAKE CITY. ON ONE SIDE IS THE MOTTO "HOLINESS TO
THE LORD," WITH THE EMBLEM OF THE PRIESTHOOD (CROWN)
OVER THE ALL-SEEING EYE. ON THE REVERSE OF THIS COIN
WERE TWO CLASPED HANDS, INITIALS GSLCPG (GREAT SALT
LAKE CITY PURE GOLD), TWO AND HALF DO (TWO AND HALF
DOLLARS), AND THE DATE 1849. COURTESY MUSEUM OF
CHURCH HISTORY AND ART, SALT LAKE CITY.

into tears and sitting down like a child. We are here! Thank the
Almighty God of Israel! . . . From the days of Oliver Cowdery
and Parley Pratt went over boundary of Jackson County [1831]
Joseph Smith had longed to be here. . . . They would not let us
come and at last we have accomplished it. We are in the midst of
the Lamanites! We are here thank the Almighty God. Glory to
the Lord . . . for here is the place of beginning."[20]

That the land was sacred and truly a promised land given by
the Lord to the Saints is not better expressed than in a talk
Brigham gave to the Saints in June 1855: "How long have we
got to live before we find out that we have nothing to conse-
crate to the Lord—that all belongs to the Father in heaven;
that these mountains are His; the valleys, the timber, the water,

the soil; in fine, the earth and its fulness?"[21] Brigham was satisfied that the Great Basin was the place, as he noted later: "We have been kicked out of the frying-pan into the fire, out of the fire into the middle of the floor, and here we are and here we will stay. God . . . will temper the elements for the good of His Saints; He will rebuke the frost and the sterility of the soil, and the land shall become fruitful."[22] The desert would blossom as a rose and the new promised land was "a good place to make Saints."[23]

The Saints were not in Salt Lake Valley very long before visitors started to stream into the newly established settlement in the Great Basin. Among them was Captain Howard Stansbury. He had been given a specific mission by the U.S. Government to provide a technical survey of a mile-by-mile examination of the Great Salt Lake and Utah valleys. During an extended stay in the City of the Saints during the winter of 1849–50, Stansbury developed a friendly relationship with forty-eight-year-old Brigham. He recalled: "Upon the personal character of the leader of this singular people, it may not, perhaps, be proper for me to comment in a communication like the present. I may nevertheless be pardoned for saying, that to me, President Young appeared to be a man of clear, sound sense, fully alive to the responsibilities of the station he occupies, sincerely devoted to the good name and interests of the people over which he presides, sensitively jealous of the least attempt to undervalue or misrepresent them, and indefatigable in devising ways and means for their moral, mental, and physical elevation. He appeared to possess the unlimited personal and official confidence of his people; while both he and his two counsellors, forming the presidency of the church, seemed to have but one object in view, the prosperity and peace of the society over which they presided."[24]

During the first general conference of the decade in April 1850 Brigham said, "Let us spend a few days and worship—the heavens are full of days and we have nothing to do but enjoy them."[25]

Above: BRIGHAM YOUNG, BY MARSENA CANNON, 12 DECEMBER 1850. TAKEN IN THE OLD PIONEER FORT BY MARSENA CANNON ABOUT THE TIME BRIGHAM LEARNED OF HIS APPOINTMENT AS THE NEW TERRITORIAL GOVERNOR. COURTESY LDS CHURCH ARCHIVES, SALT LAKE CITY.

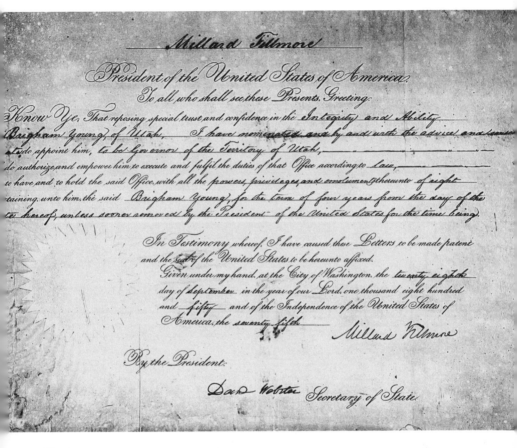

Above: BRIGHAM YOUNG'S GOVERNOR CERTIFICATE SIGNED BY U.S. PRESIDENT MILLARD FILLMORE AND SECRETARY OF STATE DANIEL WEBSTER, DATED 28 SEPTEMBER 1850. COURTESY UTAH STATE HISTORICAL SOCIETY, SALT LAKE CITY.

U.S. President Millard Fillmore appointed Brigham as the first governor of the new Utah Territory on 20 September 1850. However, Brigham did not learn of the appointment till several months later. On 3 February 1851 he officially took the oath of office.

Utah Territory
Great Salt Lake City

I Brigham Young Governor of said Territory

do solemnly swear, that I will support the Constitution of the United States,
and perform the duties pertaining to the Office of Governor of Utah Territory,
according to the best of my skill and abilities.

So help me God

Subscribed and sworn to, before me,
this third day of February A.D. 1851

Brigham Young

Daniel H. Wells
Chief Justice. Deseret

Above: BRIGHAM YOUNG'S OATH OF OFFICE, 3 FEBRUARY 1851. COURTESY LDS CHURCH ARCHIVES, SALT LAKE CITY.

Left: GOLD CANE HEAD, A GIFT FROM THE UTAH TERRITORIAL DELEGATE TO CONGRESS, WILLIAM H. HOOPER. COURTESY MUSEUM OF CHURCH HISTORY AND ART, SALT LAKE CITY.

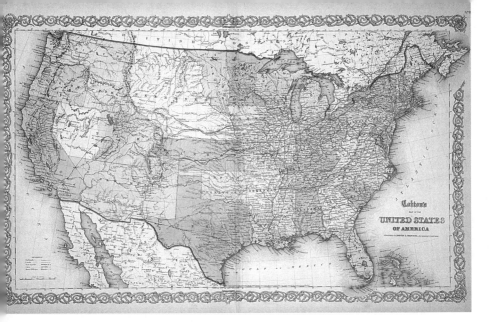

Above: 1850 MAP OF THE UNITED STATES. THE MAP SHOWS THE BOUNDARIES FOR THE TERRITORY OF UTAH ESTABLISHED BY CONGRESS IN THE COMPROMISE OF 1850. COURTESY R. Q. AND SUSAN SHUPE, SAN JUAN CAPISTRANO, CALIFORNIA.

NOTES

1. Reconstructed from two versions of minutes of the meeting; "Church Minutes," 12 February 1849, LDS Church Archives, Salt Lake City (hereafter cited as LDSCA).

2. Wilford Woodruff Journal, 17 July 1844; see Scott G. Kenney, ed., *Wilford Woodruff's Journal, 1833–1898,* 9 vols. (Midvale: Signature Books, 1983–85), 2:423.

3. *Journal of Discourses* 3:51.

4. Lyman Omer Littlefield, *Reminiscences of Latter-day Saints* (Logan: The Utah Journal Co., Printers, 1888), 166–67.

5. Brigham Young to Vilate Young, 11 August 1844, Brigham Young Papers, LDSCA.

6. Brigham Young Journal, 24 January 1845, Brigham Young Papers, LDSCA.

7. *Times and Seasons* 5 (1 January 1845): 761.

8. For a completed copy of these edited minutes, see Jeni Broberg Holzapfel and Richard Neitzel Holzapfel, eds., *A Woman's View: Helen Mar Whitney's Reminiscences of Early Church History* (Provo: Religious Studies Center, Brigham Young University, 1997), 276.

9. Journal History, 28 September 1846, LDSCA.

10. Doctrine and Covenants 136.

11. Doctrine and Covenants 136:1.

12. See Doctrine and Covenants 136:2, 4.

13. Exodus 18:21.

14. Doctrine and Covenants 136:21.

15. Doctrine and Covenants 136:22.

16. Wilford Woodruff Journal, 28 July 1847; see Kenney, ed., *Wilford Woodruff's Journal* 3:239.

17. *Journal of Discourses* 1:133.

18. Exodus 28:36–38.

19. Zechariah 14:20–21.

20. "General Church Minutes, 24 September 1848," LDSCA.

21. *Journal of Discourses* 2:308.

22. Sermon quoted in James S. Brown, *Life of a Pioneer* (Salt Lake City: Geo. Q. Cannon & Sons, 1900), 121–22.

23. *Journal of Discourses* 4:32.

24. Howard Stansbury, *Exploration and Survey of the Valley of the Great Salt Lake* (Washington, D.C.: Smithsonian Institute, 1988), 133–34.

25. *Millennial Star* 12 (1 September 1850): 260.

~~

Chapter 6
CHALLENGES AND PROGRESS

While rumors abounded about the Church's marriage practices, it was not until 1852 that Brigham presided at a meeting in Salt Lake City where the revelation recorded by Joseph Smith in 1842 that outlined the doctrine of plural marriage was publicly read. This particular Church announcement was reported wide and far throughout the world, and soon plural marriage and Brigham became inseparably connected.

Not only was Brigham's name becoming well known, but his visual likeness was also being printed for an audience hungry to know what the Mormon prophet looked like.

The year 1853 was an important one for Brigham. On Valentine's Day, 14 February, he broke ground for the Salt Lake Temple. A few months later, on 6 April, he presided over the laying of the cornerstones for the temple. He closed the services by blessing the people: "Brethren and Sisters, I bless you in the name of Jesus Christ of Nazareth, and pray my Father in Heaven to encircle you in the arms of his love and mercy, and protect us until we have finished this Temple, received the fulness of our endowments therein, and built many more."[1]

Heber C. Kimball
BORN JUNE 14TH 1801.

Brigham Young
BORN JUNE 1ST 1801.

Willard Richards,
BORN JUNE 24TH 1804.

Orson Hyde
BORN JANY 8TH 1805.

P. P. Pratt
BORN APRIL 12TH 1807.

Orson Pratt
BORN SEPTY 19TH 1811.

Wilford Woodruff
BORN MARCH 1ST 1807.

John Taylor
BORN APRIL 1ST 1808.

Geo. A. Smith,
BORN JUNE 26TH 1817.

Amasa Lyman
BORN MARCH 30TH 1813.

Ezra T. Benson
BORN FEBY 22ND 1811.

Charles C. Rich
BORN AUGT 21ST 1809.

Lorenzo Snow
BORN APRIL 3RD 1814.

Erastus Snow
BORN NOVR 9TH 1818.

Franklin D. Richards,
BORN APRIL 2ND 1821.

This Plate of the FIRST PRESIDENCY and TWELVE APOSTLES,
of the Church of Jesus Christ of Latter day Saints,
is respectfully dedicated to PRESIDENT BRIGHAM YOUNG,
by the Publishers.

Ent'd at Stationers Hall

Published by S. W. Richards &c.
15, Wilton Street Liverpool 1853

Left: THE FIRST PRESIDENCY AND TWELVE APOSTLES, BY FREDERICK PIERCY, 1 JANUARY 1853. PIERCY'S FAMOUS ILLUSTRATION OF "THE FIRST PRESIDENCY AND TWELVE APOSTLES OF THE CHURCH OF JESUS CHRIST OF LATTER-DAY SAINTS" WAS PRINTED IN JANUARY 1853 IN ENGLAND. COURTESY LDS CHURCH ARCHIVES, SALT LAKE CITY.

The eastern United States got one of its first views of Brigham in the 3 January 1854 edition of the *Gleason's Pictorial Drawing-Room Companion*. The magazine also furnished a brief overview of the Church's history, including information on Brigham:

"The Mormons. The territory of Utah is well known as the residence of the sect called the Mormons. This communion was first organized in 1830, under Joseph Smith at Kirtland, Ohio. After a temporary establishment there, it was removed to Jackson county, Missouri, thence to Caldwell county, and afterward to Illinois, where they founded the city of Nauvoo. Here they flourished for several years, when a strong public excitement was raised against them, and they resolved to

Below: SALT LAKE TEMPLE GROUND-BREAKING SERVICES, BY WILLIAM A. SMITH, 14 FEBRUARY 1853. COURTESY LDS CHURCH ARCHIVES, SALT LAKE CITY.

Above: BRIGHAM AND MARGARET PIERCE YOUNG, CA. 1851. ONE OF TWO KNOWN PHOTOGRAPHS OF BRIGHAM YOUNG POSING WITH A SPOUSE. THIS IS A COPY OF A DAGUERREOTYPE ORIGINALLY TAKEN BY MARSENA CANNON IN SALT LAKE CITY. MARGARET PIERCE MARRIED BRIGHAM YOUNG IN JANUARY 1845 AND BORE HIM ONE SON—BRIGHAM MORRIS YOUNG, IN 1854. COURTESY LDS CHURCH ARCHIVES, SALT LAKE CITY.

abandon Nauvoo, and find an asylum elsewhere. After various changes they finally located themselves in the valley of the great Salt Lake, and the nucleus was formed by them of the present territory of Utah. In 1850, Brigham Young, a portrait of whom is here given, was appointed territorial governor by Congress.

"Young is the present leader of the Mormon community, and the country is rapidly filling up with emigrants from every part of the world, but principally from the Welsh counties of England, where Mormonism has made a very deep impression. The city of the Great Salt Lake, the head-quarters of the Mormon community, stands in the lower valley of the Jordan, about twenty miles from the lake. It is laid out upon a magnif-

Right: BRIGHAM
YOUNG, CA. 1854;
ILLUSTRATION IN
*GLEASON'S PICTOR-
IAL DRAWING-ROOM
COMPANION.* COUR-
TESY R. Q. AND
SUSAN SHUPE, SAN
JUAN CAPISTRANO,
CALIFORNIA.

BRIGHAM YOUNG, THE MORMON PRESIDENT.

icent scale, being nearly four miles in length and three in breadth. The municipal regulations as to building and streets are of a sagacious character, and if followed out, will make the city a beautiful location. It is surrounded by scenery of agreeable, picturesque variety; on the northern confines a warm spring arises from the base of the mountains, the water from which is conducted by pipes into the city, while an unfailing stream of pure water flows through the city, and is made to traverse every street."[2]

Soon, travelers beyond the English-speaking world came to Zion to visit one of the most famous religious leaders of his time.

After the completion of the Beehive House and the offices of the Church President and territorial governor, most visitors

Above: Beehive House, Louis R. Chaffin, ca. 1855. The earliest known photograph of the Beehive House is this daguerreotype taken by Mr. Chaffin, one of Marsena Cannon's companions, at about the time of its completion. The wooden beehive atop the house, a Utah pioneer symbol of industry, gave the home its name. The pine-wood and sun-dried adobe house was designed by Truman O. Angell. To the left of the house are the offices for Brigham Young as governor (note sign above first door to the left) and as Church President (note sign over second door). Additionally a sign was placed over the President's office, "Tithing Office." The Lion House, Brigham Young's largest house, is shown prior to its 1856 completion. Notice that the lion is not yet on the portico. Courtesy LDS Church Archives, Salt Lake City.

held their interviews in the buildings that are still standing in Salt Lake City.

Brigham spoke to the Saints at the beginning of the October 1857 General Conference regarding the handcart pioneers on their way into the valley:

"I wish the most strict attention of the entire congregation. . . . I will now give this people the subject and the text for the Elders who may speak to-day and during the Conference, it is this, on the 5th day of October, 1856, many of our brethren

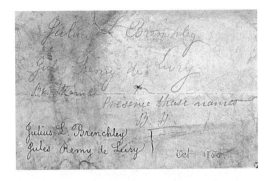

Right: JULES REMY AND
JULIUS BRENCHLEY'S
CALLING CARD. FRENCH-
MAN REMY AND ENG-
LISHMAN BRENCHLEY
SPENT A MONTH IN
UTAH AND MET WITH
BRIGHAM YOUNG ON AT
LEAST FOUR OCCASIONS.
LATER THEY PUBLISHED
THEIR IMPRESSION IN
VOYAGE AU PAYS DES MORMONS (PARIS: E. DENTU, 1860). COURTESY LDS

and sisters are on the Plains with hand-carts, and probably many are now seven hundred miles from this place, and they must be brought here, we must send assistance to them. The text will be—to get them here! I want the brethren who may speak to understand that their text is the people on the Plains, and the subject matter for this community is to send for them and bring them in before the winter sets in. That is my religion; that is the dictation of the Holy Ghost that I possess, it is to save the people. . . . This is the salvation I am now seeking for, to save our brethren that would be apt to perish, or suffer extremely, if we do not send them assistance. I shall call upon the Bishops this day, I shall not wait until to-morrow, nor until next day, for sixty good mule teams and twelve or fifteen wagons."[3]

Former Mormon turned anti-Mormon T. B. H. Stenhouse noted years later his impressions of Brigham's efforts in the handcart rescue and admitted frankly that it was Brigham's finest hour: "When news reached Brigham Young, . . . he did all that man could do to save the remnant and relieve the sufferers. Never in his whole career did he shine so gloriously in the eyes of the people. There was nothing spared that he could contribute or command. In the Tabernacle, he was 'the Lion of the Lord.'"[4]

Above: "The Hand-Cart Emigrants in a Storm," from T. B. H. Sten-house's 1873 *The Rocky Mountain Saints: A Full and complete History of the Mormons* (New York: D. Appleton and Company, 1873).

In November, after the rescue efforts had been several weeks under way, members of the Martin Company were about to enter Salt Lake City. Brigham arose and told the Saints:

"I have a few words to say, before this meeting is brought to a close. We expect that the last hand-cart company, br. Martin's will soon be in the streets by the Council House. What preparations the Bishops have made for their comfortable reception and temporary disposal I know not, but I know what I desire and am going to tell it to the people.

"When those persons arrive I do not want to see them put into houses by themselves; I want to have them distributed in this city among the families that have good and comfortable houses; and I wish the sisters now before me, and all who know how and can, to nurse and wait upon the new comers and prudently administer medicine and food to them. To speak upon these things is a part of my religion, for it pertains to taking care of the Saints.

". . . The afternoon meeting will be omitted, for I wish the sisters to go home and prepare to give those [immigrants] who have just arrived a mouthful of something to eat, and to wash

Right: BRIGHAM
YOUNG, BY
MARSENA CANNON,
CA. 1857. THE
AMBROTYPE, TAKEN
ABOUT THE TIME OF
THE UTAH WAR, RE-
VEALS AS MUCH AS
ANY WRITTEN DOCU-
MENT COULD THE
STRESS AND BURDEN
GOVERNOR AND
PRESIDENT YOUNG
EXPERIENCED WHEN
THE FEDERAL GOV-
ERNMENT "INVADED"
UTAH. COURTESY
SPECIAL COLLEC-
TIONS-MANUSCRIPTS,
J. WILLARD MAR-
RIOTT LIBRARY,
UNIVERSITY OF UTAH,
SALT LAKE CITY.

them and nurse them up. You know that I would give more for a dish of pudding and milk, or a baked potato and salt, were I in the situation of those persons who have just come in, than I would for all your prayers, though you were to stay here all the afternoon and pray. Prayer is good, but when baked potatoes and pudding and milk are needed, prayer will not supply their place on this occasion; give every duty its proper time and place."[5]

In a talk delivered on 26 July 1857 Brigham reflected on the rumors and accusations about him that were spreading across the nation in print as well as by word of mouth. "What is now the news circulated throughout the United States? That Captain Gunnison was killed by Brigham Young, and that Babbitt was killed on the Plains by Brigham Young and his Danite band. What more? . . . According to their version, I am guilty

Left. Brigham Young illustration from 10 October 1857 edition of the *Harper's Weekly*. This illustration appeared with an article, "Scenes in an American Harem." Courtesy Gary L. and Carol B. Bunker, Orem, Utah.

of the death of every man, woman, and child that has died between the Missouri river and the California gold mines."6

As the nation at large waited to hear news of the invasion of Utah, the army itself moved closer to Salt Lake City and then was forced to winter in Wyoming. It was during this period that Brigham received a blessing under the hands of his brother John, a blessing of comfort and reassurance from the Lord:

"Brother Brigham, In the name of the Lord Jesus Christ I lay my hands upon your head and bless you in the name of Israel's God, and you shall be blest from this time henceforth and forever. I seal upon your head the blessings which were given to you by our natural Father. You are a lawful heir according to the promises made over unto the Fathers, for you are a literal descendant of Joseph through the loins of Ephraim, and have a right to the blessings of the everlasting gospel and to the fulness of the priesthood, the power of which shall rest upon you henceforth and forever. Your mind shall expand, the visions of the heavens shall be opened before you that you may comprehend the fulness of the truths of heaven. You are blest with many great and precious blessings, for the Lord has had his eye upon you, and you are a chosen vessel to bear the weight of the kingdom and the vessels of the Lord, to stand as a mighty man upon the earth.

"Thou shalt be qualified for all the duties which thou art or ever shall be called to perform; thou shalt be blest with knowledge, wisdom and understanding; the revelations of Jesus shall be with you; you shall have power to control yourself, your household, and to manage all the affairs of the Church of Jesus Christ agreeably to the mind of the heavens, in connection with those that are associated with you, and no power shall overcome you; you never shall fall by the hand of an enemy for that is not the mind of the Spirit, but the mind of the Lord is that you shall escape, and be able to circumscribe the wisdom of the world. You shall be able to administer the words of eternal life to the saints, and of eternal death to your enemies, and the time shall come when the great men of the Earth who think themselves wise shall seek unto you for knowledge and safety, and you shall have power over them, and the time also shall come when you shall not only have power over the United States, but over the Nations of the earth, and you shall do a mighty work, your name shall be honorable, you shall rise in the scale of intelligence until you become associated with the Gods. From your loins Apostles, Prophets and Kings shall spring; your posterity, shall be very numerous, even as the sands of the Sea, and they shall call you blessed, and you shall bless them.

"Be of good cheer, for thou shalt always have strength according to thy day. Notwithstanding your enemies may hunt you like a Roe upon the mountains yet you shall escape as the bird from the hands of the Fowler, and not a hair of your head shall fall, but you shall be sustained in all times and places, and you shall yet converse with the Lord as did the brother of Jared; you shall do the work whereunto the Lord has called you, and that is to establish righteousness and truth.

"I confer upon you the blessings of the heavens and of the earth; you shall be blest in your family, be able to administer

Left: Brigham Young, July 1858, by Marsena Cannon. A copy of a daguerreotype purportedly taken in the Beehive House in July 1858, shortly after Brigham returned to Salt Lake from the "Move South" on 30 June 1858. Courtesy LDS Church Archives, Salt Lake City.

health and life to the afflicted. If you keep humble, which you will, you shall have a fulness of joy, live on the earth many years, even till your head is white as the pure wool or as snow, and your mouth shall continue to speak words of life to thousands and millions of the inhabitants of the earth, who shall rejoice to hear your voice. You shall come forth in the first resurrection, be numbered with the great and good, with Joseph the Prophet and Seer, and all that innumerable company and the blood washed throng [sic] which no man could number.

"This is thy lot, brother Brigham, therefore be glad and rejoice, for thou canst have these and every other blessing, privilege and mercy thy heart may desire in righteousness. The Spirit of God like a river shall be bestowed upon you continually, because you have walked uprightly before the Lord in the days of your youth; you have also past through sorrow and grief, and made sacrifices for the kingdom of heaven's sake, therefore all is yours, and I seal them upon you in the name of the Father, Son and Holy Ghost, even so: Amen."[7]

In September, Brigham and Lucy's son Feramorz Young was born. Several months later Brigham blessed him: "Feramorz in the name of the Lord Jesus Christ we lay our hands upon thee and bless thee according to the order of the Holy Priesthood; and ask our Father to pour out of his Spirit upon you, heal up your body, and bless you abundantly. We bless you with all the blessings of Abraham Isaac and Jacob, and say live, and have power over death and disease, and foul spirits, and we seal upon you the blessing of life, and health, with the full use of your mental faculties; and also seal upon you the power of the Holy Priesthood which shall rest upon you from your faith, and say be thou blessed, and thy mind shall be quick and open to receive the things of God. Thou shall be preserved in the hour of dangers for the angel of the Lord shall guide and bear thee up that thou shalt not be destroyed, but live to be a mighty instrument in the hands of the Lord of doing good to the House of Israel, in gathering their remnants to Zion; and thou shall become a saviour upon Mount Zion to save the house of Esau, and all blessings pertaining to life and salvation—pertaining to this world and to the world to come, and in the eternal priesthood we seal upon you in the name of Lord Jesus Christ, Amen."[8]

As the nation began to focus upon the problems of sectionalism in the East, Brigham still received attention in the newspapers and magazines of the day. He noted in April 1859: "Don't fret your gizzard over that. I care nothing about my character in the world. I do not care what men say about me. I want my character to stand fair in the eyes of my Heavenly Father."[9]

The 3 September 1859 *Harper's Weekly* contained Horace Greeley's interview with Brigham in Salt Lake City. Greeley, editor of the New York *Tribune,* conducted a two-hour interview with fifty-eight-year-old Brigham on 13 July 1859 that captured national attention as the two discussed plural marriage, slavery, and Mormon doctrine. The "Two Hours with Brigham Young" is reportedly the "first full-fledged modern

HARPER'S WEEKLY.

A JOURNAL OF CIVILIZATION.

Vol. III.—No. 140.]   NEW YORK, SATURDAY, SEPTEMBER 3, 1859.   [Price Five Cents.

Entered according to Act of Congress, in the Year 1859, by Harper & Brothers, in the Clerk's Office of the District Court for the Southern District of New York.

BRIGHAM YOUNG'S RELIGION, WEALTH, WIVES, ETC.

THE accompanying illustration will convey to the beholder some idea of a very remarkable interview which took place a few days since between Brigham Young, the chief of the Mormons, and Horace Greeley, the Editor of the New York *Tribune*. Mr. Greeley, on his way across the continent by the overland route, stopped at Salt Lake City, and there fell in with an old acquaintance, Dr. Bernhisel, who was for some time Mormon delegate in Congress. The Doctor proposed to introduce Mr. Greeley to Governor Young, and the offer, as may be imagined, was gladly accepted. We give the rest in Mr. Greeley's own language, simply observing that Brigham Young's statements are the latest and most authentic expositions we have of the Mormon doctrine:

We were very cordially welcomed at the door by the President, who led us into the second-story parlor of the largest of his houses (he has three), where I was introduced to Heber C. Kimball, General Wells, General Ferguson, Albert Carrington, Elias Smith, and several other leading men to the Church, with two full-grown sons of the President. After some unimportant conversation on general topics, I stated that I had come in quest of fuller knowledge respecting the doctrines and polity of the Mormon Church; and would like to ask some questions bearing directly on these, if there were no objection. President Young avowed his willingness to respond to all pertinent inquiries. The conversation proceeded substantially as follows:

THE RELIGION OF MORMON.

GREELEY. "Am I to regard Mormonism (so-called) as a new religion, or is simply a new development of Christianity?"

BRIGHAM. "We hold that there can be no true Christian Church without a priesthood directly commissioned by, and in immediate communication with, the Son of God and Saviour of mankind. Such a Church is that of the Latter-Day Saints, called by their enemies Mormons. We know no other that even pretends to have present and direct revelations of God's will."

GREELEY. "Then I am to understand that you regard all other Churches professing to be Christian as the Church of Rome regards all Churches not in communion with itself—as schismatic, heretical, and out of the way of salvation?"

BRIGHAM. "Yes, substantially."

GREELEY. "Apart from this, in what respect do your doctrines differ essentially from those of our orthodox Protestant Churches—the Baptist or Methodist, for example?"

BRIGHAM. "We hold the doctrine of Christianity, as revealed in the Old and New Testaments; also in the Book of Mormon, which teaches the same cardinal truths, and those only."

GREELEY. "Do you believe in a personal devil—a distinct, conscious, spiritual being, whose nature and acts are essentially malignant and evil?"

BRIGHAM. "We do."

GREELEY. "Do you hold the doctrine of Eternal Punishment?"

BRIGHAM. "We do: though perhaps not exactly as other Churches do. We believe it as the Bible teaches it."

GREELEY. "I understand that you regard Baptism by Immersion as essential?"

BRIGHAM. "We do."

GREELEY. "Do you practice Infant Baptism?"

BRIGHAM. "No."

GREELEY. "Do you make removal to these valleys obligatory on your converts?"

BRIGHAM. "They would consider themselves greatly aggrieved if they were not invited thither. We hold to such a gathering together of God's people as the Bible

foretells, and that this is the place and now is the time appointed for its commencement."

GREELEY. "The predictions to which you refer have usually, I think, been understood to indicate Jerusalem (or Judea) as the place of such gathering?"

BRIGHAM. "Yes, for the Jews; not for others."

HOW THE BISHOPS AND PRIESTS LIVE.

GREELEY. "Let me now be enlightened with regard more especially to your Church polity. I understand that you require each member to pay over one-tenth of all he produces or earns to the Church?"

BRIGHAM. "That is a requirement of our faith. There is no compulsion as to the payment. Each member sets in the premises according to his pleasure, under the dictates of his own conscience."

GREELEY. "What is done with the proceeds of this tithing?"

BRIGHAM. "Part of it is devoted to building temples and other places of worship; part to helping the poor and needy converts on their way to this county; and the largest portion to the support of the poor among the Saints."

GREELEY. "Is none of it paid to bishops and other dignitaries of the Church?"

BRIGHAM. "Not one penny. No bishop, no elder, no deacon, or other Church officer, receives any compensation for his official services. A bishop is often required to put his hand in his own pocket and provide therefrom for the poor of his charge; but he never receives any thing for his services."

GREELEY. "How, then, do your ministers live?"

BRIGHAM. "By the labor of their own hands, like the first Apostles. Every bishop, every elder, may be daily seen at work in the field or the shop, like his neighbors; every minister of the Church has his proper calling by which he earns the bread of his family; he who can not or will not do the Church's work for nothing is not wanted in her service; even our lawyers (pointing to General Ferguson and another present, who are the regular lawyers of the Church) are paid nothing for their services.

BRIGHAM CONSIDERS HIMSELF A MILLIONAIRE.

"I am the only person in the Church who has not a regular calling apart from the Church's service, and I never received one farthing from her treasury. If I obtain any thing from the tithing-house, I am charged with and pay for it, just as any one else would; the clerks in the tithing-store are paid like other clerks, but no one is ever paid for any service pertaining to the ministry. We think a man who can not make his living aside from the ministry of Christ unsuited to that office. I am called rich, and consider myself worth $250,000; but no dollar of it was ever paid me by the Church, or for any service as a minister of the Everlasting Gospel. I lost nearly all I had when we were broken up in Missouri and driven from that State; I was nearly stripped again when Joseph Smith was murdered and we were driven from Illinois; but nothing was ever made up to me by the Church, nor by any one. I believe I know how to acquire property, and how to take care of it."

COMPARES THE MORMONS TO THE APOSTLES, AND BUCHANAN TO PONTIUS PILATE.

GREELEY. "Can you give me any rational explanation of the aversion and hatred with which your people are generally regarded by those among whom they have lived, and with whom they have been brought directly in contact?"

BRIGHAM. "No other explanation then is afforded by the crucifixion of Christ, and the kindred treatment of God's ministers, prophets, and saints in all ages."

HOW ABOUT POLYGAMY?

GREELEY. "With regard, then, to the grave question on which your doctrines and practices are avowedly at war with those of the Christian world—that of a plurality of wives—is the system of your Church acceptable to the majority of the women?"

BRIGHAM. "They could not be more averse to it than I was when it was first revealed to us as the Divine

INTERVIEW BETWEEN BRIGHAM YOUNG AND HON. HORACE GREELEY AT SALT LAKE CITY.

Left: BRIGHAM YOUNG AND HORACE GREELEY ILLUSTRATION; *HARPER'S WEEKLY* 3 SEPTEMBER 1859. LEFT TO RIGHT: BRIGHAM YOUNG AND HORACE GREELEY. COURTESY R. Q. AND SUSAN SHUPE, SAN JUAN CAPISTRANO, CALIFORNIA.

interview with a well-known public figure printed in an American newspaper." Greeley's dispatch first appeared in the New York *Tribune* for August 20, 1859 (an issue that probably sold more copies than any previous issue) and a few weeks later in *Harper's Weekly.*

In March 1860 Brigham told the Saints: "The last time I spoke to you here I told you that I found my religion just as sweet to me in my private capacity, in my secret meditations upon my bed, and in my closet, in my office, or with my family, as it is when I am in this stand. I love it as well—esteem it as highly; it is as precious to my understanding, and it invigorates, buoys up, strengthens, and fills every power of my capacity with unspeakable joy, just as much at home as it does here. I hope this is the case with you all."[10]

Probably one of the most significant events of the year occurred on 25 August 1860: "George Quayle Cannon was ordained a member of the Quorum of the Twelve Apostles of the Church of Jesus Christ of Latter-day Saints, under the hands of Presidents Brigham Young, Heber C. Kimball, and Daniel H. Wells and Elders John Taylor, George A. Smith, Wilford Woodruff, and Franklin D. Richards, President Brigham Young being mouth."[11]

Plagued with persistent dental problems, Brigham finally had Dr. Dunyon pull five teeth on 28 April 1862, "being all the remaining teeth he had left in his head. The President is getting a new set of teeth."[12] This not only affected his facial features (easily detected in the photographic record) but also caused him some discomfort and embarrassment from time to time. Yet he was able to keep a positive attitude about the whole thing, as an experience at the St. George home of Erastus Snow demonstrates.

BRIGHAM YOUNG.

BRIGHAM YOUNG, the President and Chief Prophet of the Church of the Latter Day Saints, or Mormons, was born about the year 1800. Very little is known of his early life. It is generally supposed that he is a native of the State of Ohio; and it is said that he has brothers engaged in the ministry in the Methodist Church. In connection with the Mormons he first appeared in a prominent position in August, 1844, soon after the murder of Joseph Smith, the founder of the sect. Young was then President of the Twelve Apostles, and in that capacity signed a letter addressed "To the Church of Jesus Christ of Latter Day Saints in Nauvoo (Illinois) and all the World." One of the principal men in the community, Sydney Rigdon, sought to succeed Smith; but charges of heresy and improper conduct were urged against him by Young and others: he was excommunicated, and Young was appointed the successor of Smith. By his shrewdness and great natural ability he has shown the wisdom of the choice. Perceiving that the Illinoisians were hostile to his people, he planned and carried out an exodus unparalleled in history for the sufferings of the people who accomplished it. They resolved to place the Rocky Mountains between them and persecuting Christendom. Cold and hunger killed many on the road; but, after a year and a half of inconceivable hardships, the pioneers reached the Valley of the Great Salt Lake, in July, 1847, and founded a settlement. The mass of the people followed in the next year, and in the thirteen years which have succeeded, under the guidance and government of Brigham Young, they have converted a bare valley into a lovely region of cultivated fields, rich orchards, flower-filled gardens, and pleasant residences. They have brought the water from the hills in sparkling rivulets through every street. They have erected mills for grinding the grain of their own growth, and sawing the wood that their own sturdy arms have felled. They manufacture their own paper, and spin and weave their own fabrics; and when articles are wanted from the outer world they are carried across the great desert in waggons, sometimes numbering over fifty in a single train. In all these works "the President," as the people call him, or "Brother Brigham," as he styles himself, has been the directing and influencing power. He has forbidden the establishment of beershops, and there is only one place in Salt Lake City where liquor in quantities can be obtained. Soon after sunset the streets are as quiet as Goldsmith's Deserted Village, for the citizens remain in their homes, except when in the winter they attend the balls or theatrical entertainments, which are frequent, or exercise their voices in their musical parties. A traveller ignorant of their practice of polygamy would say from the appearance of things that a more industrious and better-conducted community is not to be found. They consider polygamy, to the extent of having five wives at least, an essential of respectability; but the practice is by no means universal. Young is President by semi-annual election, or rather by a unanimous vivâ voce confirmation by the people assembled in the Bowery. He rules, as head of the Church and *de facto* Governor of the territory of Utah, over a region containing more than 180,000 square miles prior to the formation by the last Congress of the new territories, which have slightly infringed upon his domain. This is an extent of country exceeding the size of Great Britain and Ireland by over 70,000 square miles. Young is a portly man of middle height, now in his sixty-second year, and apparently so healthy that he may live for some years yet to direct the destinies of the 70,000 who are said to reside in Utah.

BRIGHAM YOUNG'S RESIDENCE.

The residence of Brigham Young is on the northern side of Salt Lake City, on a declivity above which the foothills of the Wahsatch Mountains rise. In the View his house is nearly in the centre, and is surrounded by a small square tower with a golden beehive on the top, the emblem of the city. In this building, which is of timber, his first wife and family reside. The low building on the left contains the offices of the church. Next on the left, the principal object in the picture, is the Lion House, where the remainder of his wives reside. Some say there are twenty of these spiritual wives, others say sixty-one, one for each year of his life. A smaller (round) tower to the left of the turret on the house surmounts the schoolhouse, a neat edifice, in which the children only of Brigham Young and Heber Kimball are educated. The white house on the right of Brigham's was the first erected for him in Salt Lake City, and is now the home of his eldest son and designated successor, Joseph Young. The buildings on the extreme left in the View are garden houses, offices, and residences of some of the wives. A wall of earth and stones incloses a large piece of ground, and surrounds Young's and Kimball's premises and gardens. In the lower portion of the Engraving, on the right, is a portion of the residence of Bishop Wells.

The View and the Portrait are from photographs taken recently by C. R. Savage, late of Southampton, and were brought from Salt Lake City by a gentleman who spent several days there early in September.

BRIGHAM YOUNG, PRESIDENT AND CHIEF PROPHET OF THE MORMON CHURCH.

SHERWOOD WORKS, BATTERSEA.

IN 1849 we engraved Price's Patent Candle Company's Works at Vauxhall, and in 1854 those near Birkenhead. We now, as illustrating the growth of yearly chemical manufactures in this country, give an Engraving in connection with the nearly-completed works of this firm at Battersea.

The site of a great part of these works was in 1843 a beautiful garden, with a terrace on the bank of the Thames where George IV. and Mrs. Fitzherbert used formerly to walk. A letter written by the managing director, who showed us over the works, to a brother in India, dated December, 1843, gives the estimate for putting up the new factory as £500, and of its hands as being required to work it. Now the works extend over eleven acres, of which some six are roofed over; the capital invested in apparatus and buildings is about £200,000, and, in spite of every effort to work by means of machinery, about 800 people are employed. In 1848 the price of tallow, which generally regulates that of other fats, was £41 10s. per ton, and the price of the company's now principal raw material—palm oil—under £29 per ton, while the price of composite candles was 1s. per pound. In the early part of this year (1861)

the price of tallow was £59 per ton, and of palm oil £45, while that of composite candles, not, indeed, of the best quality, but equal to the composite candles of 1848, was 9d. per pound.

This change in the external circumstances which has gradually taken place has been met by internal change in the shape of concentration of innumerable contrivances for saving loss of material in process, for saving in labour, and for improvement in products, so as to change the business from one dependent on favourable prices of particular raw materials, and on a monopoly from patents, into one resting on the broader basis of cheapened manufacture on an immense scale.

We should weary our readers by attempting to trace the steps of progress in detail, and therefore confine ourselves to a birdseye view of the works and of the candle-room, and confine our description to the greatest novelties, the new arrangements for candle-moulding, and the new manufactures from Burmese petroleum.

The candle-room, of which we give an Engraving, is 160ft. long by 100ft. wide, in which upwards of 100 tons of candles are made weekly during the busy season. The new candle-machine consists of a long row of moulds, over which a filler runs on a railway; this filler drops the melted candle material into the moulds one after the other as it reaches them. After a sufficient time has been allowed for solidifying and cooling, a number of boys move rapidly down the frames, and the candles seem to jump from their bed as if by magic, the fact being that each mould is connected to a reservoir of high-pressure air, and, on the boys turning cocks attached to the moulds, the candles are blown out. Innumerable contrivances for "drawing" candles had been attempted, as our conductor informed us, at home and abroad, but none has equalled the power of high-pressure air, which, great as it is, is so gentle as not to injure the fine polish on the moulds. We were struck by the healthy, hearty appearance of the young lads, who appear to do almost all the work of the room, and were informed that one good deed of the new machine was to abolish the necessity for night work, which under the old system could not be avoided, when making soft candles through a large part of the year, and which is for boys most objectionable. Formerly seven candle-rooms were kept working night and day, now there is but one, and that working only in the day. The new machine, however, like most great improvements, had at first its drawback: the boys required to work it coming from a new neighbourhood and with less power of

THE RESIDENCE OF BRIGHAM YOUNG AT THE GREAT SALT LAKE CITY, UTAH.

selection than was the case at Belmont, were slow to learn the use of their fingers. Wicks were occasionally on one side, and in very exceptional instances candles were even made wickless. None of us notice the number of good candles we have burnt, but we all fasten on the bad ones; and the new machine was found fault with though perfectly innocent, it having no tendency whatever to cause one-sided wicks. But the lads gradually became accustomed to their work, and the machine has now justice done to it. A rather severe test has lately been applied to make sure that due care is being taken in the adjustment of wicks—a candle-machine is stopped, and every candle is broken across to ascertain that the wick is in the centre. We were informed that 6000 candles had been lately proved in this way, with the result of only one imperfect one which could have escaped detection.

At one end of the room is a series of circular saws. This, a French plan, was explained to us as having given the means of ensuring candles made from materials of different specific gravities being of exact weight. We were glad to hear that candles are now more generally of full weight than they formerly were. The company at one time had great difficulty in some of their scrap markets, having with their pound packets of 16oz. to compete with foreign pound packets of 18oz. to 15oz. They adopted a very simple means of defence, making two sizes of packets, both labelled prominently, the one as being 16oz., the other as being 12oz. This has had, to a great extent, the effect of rescuing candle pound packets from the fate of "pint" bottles. If the public would take the trouble to see that candles they buy weigh what they profess, they would strengthen the habits of the makers of full-weight candles. Most English manufacturers, we were told, give full weight, but there are those who do not.

A large quantity of water is used in the candle-machines, which, in its course, becomes tepid. This is allowed to run into a large swimming-bath, erected at the expense of Mr. James Wilson. This bath is most popular with the boys. The exhilarating effect of bathing expresses itself so loudly that a law had to be passed that boys should only bathe in relays of forty, in the fear that one of the party might be drowned without any power of making himself heard in the general din.

In one of the machines we saw some beautiful candles called Belmontine, more transparent than spermaceti. These, we were told, were manufactured from Rangoon petroleum, to which department we then were, and saw, first, a huge vessel which holds 16-ton charges of the crude petroleum. This, as it wells out in the earth in Burmah, is a greenish-brown substance, of about the consistence of honey. The large vessel first extracts from it a colourless light fluid, having much the character of benzine, but without the unpleasant smell. This is used for cleaning dresses and furniture from stains of grease. A less volatile fluid, Belmontine oil, is next separated: this is used for lamps. Then comes a heavier oil, which enters largely into the composition of a lubricating oil, sent out in large quantities for the spindles of the great north-country mills, and for use in general machinery. Last of all comes the beautiful candle material Belmontine. These petroleum manufactures form a comparatively new and very important part of the company's trade.

It is curious to trace the changes in sources of light. First these were almost exclusively animal—sperm, seal, and southern whale oil for our lamps, and spermaceti for candles. Then came a vegetable epoch. Palm oil and cocoanut oil were much used for candles, and great quantities of rape or colza oil were used in moderator lamps. Recently we appear to have entered on a mineral era—Belmontine and paraffin oils.

The last, from numerous sources, are manufactured on an immense scale for lamps; and the manufacture of candles from Belmontine and paraffin is a very rapidly increasing one.

M. FECHTER'S OTHELLO.

THE scenic arrangements at the Princes' that so picturesquely illustrate the version of "Othello" furnished by M. Fechter to the English stage have now become such topics of criticism, curiosity, and attention that we only supply a reasonably implied public demand by enabling our readers to look for themselves on one of the scenes that have excited most approbation.

We select the opening of the second act, which represents Cyprus under the effects of a gradually abating storm, and places the spectator, as it were, on a platform before the town, looking upon the harbour. Never were Mr. Telbin's skill and taste more beautifully shown than in this well-disposed pictorial set. Lesser arrangements the observer will find in it, which come into proud use during the performance—such as a large arcade at the back of the scene, a gate on the right, and a capstan at the left corner, surrounded with bales of merchandise. These adjuncts enable the actors to shift from place to place, from the level to the platform, and from a sitting to an erect position, according to the propriety of the scene. The reader will see that the especial merit of M. Fechter's action. In pointing these out lies edition.

Attention to these small particulars, too much in general neglected on the English stage, conduces to a pleasing variety in the business of the scene. Iago sometimes on front, sometimes on the platform, sometimes on the capstan, conversing familiarly with Desdemona and Emilia, has so many points of exhibition, and every change produces a different picture. Othello's banner-bearer supports the flag embroidered with the Lion of St. Mark. A page, also, is charged with the helmet, the gauntlet, and the truncheon, which he bears on a velvet cushion.

Such adjuncts as these make the scene a pictorial composition. Such scenes, too, have another advantage—they are moving pictures. The whole setting-up may be accepted as a dramatic panorama. It is so remarkably beautiful and elegant that, whatever minute censure may be extended by captious critics to particular portions, or whatever jealousy may be indulged in by professional rivals, there can be no doubt that the English public owe a debt of thankfulness to M. Fechter for the care and attention which he has displayed in the practical application of the speculative improvements in the acting of Shakspearean drama, and which have been suggested to his creative and active intelligence by a long study of the subject. It affords us pleasure, indeed, to find that our neighbours have at length appreciated the genius of our unrivalled dramatist, and we shall not too closely examine the services they are willing to render. They are precious gifts from one people to another.

It appears that one morning Brigham was cleaning his den-
tures at the family wash bench just outside a back door when one
of the little Snow girls caught sight of him. Brigham quickly
plopped his teeth into his mouth as she stood staring in amaze-
ment. Little Flora bounced up and down pleading: "Oh, Brother
Brigham, show me your teeth! Show me your teeth, Brother
Brigham!"[13] Brigham satisfied her childhood curiosity by kindly
consenting and pulling out his teeth for her to examine.

In 1863 Brigham made one of his annual trips from Salt
Lake City to St. George. A. J. Allen, who accompanied the
President's party, noted: "May 9th Held conferance also the
10th held conferenace Bro John Taylor proffecied in the name
of the lord the people in that place should be blest and Bro.
Brigham testyfied to it also he also state that he had seen in the
vision of his mind a large citty built where St. George now
stands with towers and [steeples] one hundred and fifteen
(feet) high etc."[14] Brigham dedicated a temple there in 1877.

As had been his tradition since Nauvoo days, in 1866
Brigham met regularly in a prayer circle. On the first day of July
1866, Wilford Woodruff recorded having attended Brigham's
prayer circle that day and made note of a singular event:

"I met at the Prayer Circle with Presidet Young John Taylor W. Woodruff G. A. Smith G. Q. Cannon & Joseph F Smith.
John Taylor Prayed & President Young was mouth. At the
close of the Prayer Presidet Young arose from his knees. . . . Of
a sudden he stoped & Exclaimed hold on, 'Shall I do as I feel
led? I always fell [feel] well to do as the Spirit Constrains me. It
is my mind to Ordain Brother Joseph F Smith to the Apostle-
ship, and to be one of my Councillors.'

"He then Called upon Each one of us for an Expression of
our Feelings and we Individually responded that it met our

Left: ONE OF TWO
KNOWN PHOTO-
GRAPHIC IMAGES OF
BRIGHAM YOUNG
WITH A SPOUSE, CA.
1863. HARRIET
"AMELIA" FOLSOM
MARRIED BRIGHAM
IN JANUARY 1863.
THEY HAD NO CHIL-
DREN. COURTESY
LDS CHURCH
ARCHIVES, SALT
LAKE CITY.

Harty approval. . . . After which Brother Joseph F Smith knelt . . . we laid our hands upon him, Brother Brigham being mouth."[15]

Joseph F. Smith, son of Hyrum and Mary Fielding Smith, was twenty-seven years old at the time of his ordination. Later, on 8 October 1867, Brigham set him apart as a member of the Quorum of the Twelve, but he continued as a counselor to the First Presidency until Brigham's death in 1877.

In 1868, as the new "Iron Highway" made its way towards Utah, Brigham passed into another phase of life. On 7 August 1868 Edmund Ellsworth Jr. was born to Edmond Ellsworth and Ellen Camilla Blair. Edmond Ellsworth was Brigham's grandson, born to Elizabeth Young and Edmond Lovell Ellsworth. Brigham lived to see another twenty-one great-grandchildren born before his death in 1877.

Right: JOSEPH F. SMITH,
BY CHARLES W. CARTER,
CA. 1866. COURTESY LDS
CHURCH ARCHIVES, SALT
LAKE CITY.

In the late 1860s most Saints lived in small, quiet rural communities that spread out from Salt Lake City like spokes of a wheel. While differences could be observed between the various settlements, such as terrain and climate, most towns were remarkably similar. The local church was the physical center of the community, and the social, economic, political, and religious center as well. Wide streets were lined with Lombardy poplars, and ditches carrying water could be found on both sides of the roads. Based on Joseph Smith's plat of Zion, the community was laid out on a grid pattern, with streets running east and west and north and south from the central square, where the meetinghouse usually stood. Fences, roads, public buildings, and irrigation ditches had all been built by cooperation.

Brigham knew that the railroad would bring wonderful opportunities, especially helping in the effort to gather converts to Zion faster, easier, and less dangerously. Additionally, Brigham knew that the coming of steam would help build the Salt Lake Temple. On the other hand he also knew that the railroad would bring large numbers of non-Mormons who would be seeking to exploit the natural resources of the region, and that the Latter-day Saints' effort to be self-sufficient would thus be undermined.

Above: Painted by the first woman artist in Utah, "Brigham Young and His Friends," reminds one of the William W. Major painting "Joseph Smith and His Friends," ca. 1845. The artist, Sarah Ann Burbage Long, was an 1854 English convert and the wife of Brigham's clerk, John V. Long. From left to right: John V. Long, John Young, Edwin Woolley, George A. Smith, Lorenzo Snow, Heber C. Kimball, Brigham Young, and Daniel Wells. Behind the group are images of Jedediah M. Grant, Joseph Smith, and Hyrum Smith, and a bust of Willard Richards. Courtesy Museum of Church History and Art, Salt Lake City.

In an effort to check as much as possible the negative impact the railroad would have, Brigham revived the School of the Prophets for the men and the Relief Society for the women, and expanded the cooperative movement.

The School of the Prophets, which had originally been organized by Joseph Smith in Ohio, became a tool by which not only to teach the doctrine of the kingdom but also to help further the social, economic, and political self-sufficiency of the Saints. In a meeting held in May 1868, a clerk noted: "Prest.

Right: THEOLOGICAL LECTURES [SCHOOL OF THE PROPHETS] PASS, DATED 13 MARCH 1868. COURTESY SPECIAL COLLECTIONS, HAROLD B. LEE LIBRARY, BRIGHAM YOUNG UNIVERSITY, PROVO, UTAH.

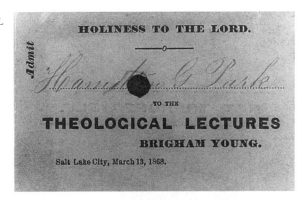

HOLINESS TO THE LORD.

Admit

Hamilton G. Park

TO THE

THEOLOGICAL LECTURES

BRIGHAM YOUNG.

Salt Lake City, March 13, 1868.

Young gave to the School of the Prophets the terms of the Railway contract and acknowledged the hand of the Lord in giving this people the privilege of performing the work; thus keeping away from our midst the swarms of scalliwags that the construction of the railway would bring here. A good influence pervaded the meeting and all seemed to feel the same. When the Prest. expressed the hope that the job might be completed creditably to the Saints, that in the halls of congress it might be announced that no part of the national highway was completed

Left: BRIGHAM YOUNG, CA. 1864; IN PRIVATE POSSESSION. ACCORDING TO THE FAMILY TRADITION THIS PAINTING WAS DONE BY A VISITING ARTIST FROM EUROPE OR THE EASTERN UNITED STATES.

Left: ILLUSTRATION FROM THE 28 JULY 1866 EDITION OF THE *FRANK LESLIE'S ILLUSTRATED NEWSPAPER.* COURTESY MUSEUM OF CHURCH HISTORY AND ART, SALT LAKE CITY.

Below: BRIGHAM YOUNG, BY CHARLES R. SAVAGE, CA. 1866. COURTESY R. Q. AND SUSAN SHUPE, SAN JUAN CAPISTRANO, CALIFORNIA.

Above: THE YOUNG BROTHERS, BY CHARLES W. CARTER, CA. 1866. LEFT TO RIGHT: LORENZO, BRIGHAM, PHINEAS, JOSEPH, AND JOHN. ALL THE MEMBERS OF THE IMMEDIATE FAMILY LIVING AT THE TIME THE CHURCH WAS ESTAB-LISHED JOINED IT AND DIED FAITHFUL MEMBERS, INCLUDING FATHER, JOHN YOUNG; SISTERS NANCY, FANNY, RHODA, SUSANNAH, AND LOUISA; AND THESE FIVE BROTHERS. COURTESY LDS CHURCH ARCHIVES, SALT LAKE CITY.

Left: BRIGHAM YOUNG, BY EDWARD MARTIN, CA. 1867. COURTESY R. Q. AND SUSAN SHUPE, SAN JUAN CAPIS-TRANO, CALIFORNIA.

WOMEN LEADERS, CA. 1880. LEFT TO RIGHT: ZINA D. H. YOUNG, EMELINE PARTRIDGE, ELIZA R. SNOW. COURTESY SPECIAL COLLECTIONS-MANUSCRIPTS, J. WILLARD MARRIOTT LIBRARY, UNIVERSITY OF UTAH, SALT LAKE CITY.

⟡

more satisfactorily, the brethren clapped their hands en masse."[16]

Eliza R. Snow, chosen as the new president of the Relief Society in 1867, moved to promote women's rights, education, and the cooperative movement. Eliza also reached out to younger women through the retrenchment associations.

Brigham had initiated the retrenchment movement in 1869 when he appointed Mary Isabella Horne to establish a semi-monthly women's meeting to promote a reform in "diet and dress." Later, Brigham organized the Young Ladies Retrenchment Association among his own daughters and planned it to be copied throughout the Mormon settlements.

Brigham made another tour in October and November 1869, visiting the Saints in Utah, Juab, and Sanpete counties. In a letter to his son, who was serving a mission in England at the time, he gave a report of the trip: "On the 26th ult. I

Right: CAROLINE "CARLIE" PARTRIDGE YOUNG, CA. 1868. BRIGHAM YOUNG'S DAUGHTER IN "RETRENCHMENT DRESS." COURTESY WINNIFRED CANNON JARDINE, SALT LAKE CITY.

⌁

Below: "PREST. B. YOUNG & PARTY ON THE COLORADO PLATEAU," BY CHARLES R. SAVAGE, 18 MARCH 1870. SEATED IN THE CENTER, LEFT TO RIGHT: JOHN P. SQUIRES (NEXT TO THE RIFLES), JOHN W. YOUNG, BRIGHAM YOUNG JR., DANIEL H. WELLS (ON THE CHAIR), UNKNOWN, BRIGHAM YOUNG, AND GEORGE A. SMITH. STANDING BEHIND CENTER ROW, LEFT TO RIGHT: (BEGINNING WITH MAN IN WHITE COAT, JUST BEHIND JOHN W. YOUNG) LORENZO DOW YOUNG, UNKNOWN, AMELIA FOLSOM YOUNG, JOHN TAYLOR, UNKNOWN, MINERVA W. SNOW (WIFE OF ERASTUS SNOW), BATHSHEBA SMITH (WIFE OF GEORGE A. SMITH). BRIGHAM YOUNG IS OFTEN MIS-IDENTIFIED IN THIS IMAGE AS THE MAN SITTING ON THE CHAIR IN THE CENTER OF THE PHOTOGRAPH. COURTESY LDS CHURCH ARCHIVES, SALT LAKE CITY.

Above: Eagle Gate, by Savage and Ottinger, ca. 1866. A State of Deseret law passed in 1851 required all land owners to fence their property as a restraint for their own livestock and a protection against their neighbors' cattle. Brigham Young therefore directed that a fence be built around his property, as can be seen in the earliest photograph of the Beehive House. Within a short period a cobblestone wall nine feet high replaced the original wood enclosure, as shown in the photograph. The much-photographed Eagle Gate was carved by English emigrant Ralph Ramsey in 1859. Assisted by fellow countryman William Bell, Ramsey utilized a design by Hiram B. Clawson, a convert from New York, business manager and son-in-law of Brigham Young. The large copper-covered wooden eagle is atop the gate to City Creek Canyon. Courtesy LDS Church Archives, Salt Lake City.

started (accompanied by some of the brethren) on a trip to the settlements. . . . The people everywhere received us with demonstrations of welcome. At Ft. Ephraim we had a grand torchlight reception, & the Chinese Canters & transparencies were very effective. Take it altogether, it was season of rejoicing. The teachings given were of a thoroughly practical character, adapted to the instruction of all, & on a variety of subjects of interest. In eleven days we travelled about 300 miles—visited 20 Settlements & held 27 meetings."[17]

On 10 January 1870 Brigham participated in the ceremonies celebrating the completion of the railroad connection to Salt Lake City from Ogden. Some 15,000 people gathered to witness the laying of the last rail and the driving of the last

Above: BRIGHAM YOUNG, BY ENOCH PERRY, 1866.
SOME TIME IN LATE 1865, ENOCH WOOD PERRY JR.
OBTAINED ANOTHER COMMISSION, THIS TIME FROM
THE CITY FATHERS OF SALT LAKE. FOR A FULL-LENGTH
LIFE-SIZE PORTRAIT OF BRIGHAM YOUNG HE WAS PAID
$1,000 IN GOLD. COURTESY THE SALT LAKE CITY AND
COUNTY BUILDING, SALT LAKE CITY.

spike by Brigham. Photographer Charles R. Savage noted: "Grand Finale to track laying Pres. B. Young drove the last spike. Many visitors came from different points. Everything passed off very lively and pleasant. Took 2 photos of the ceremony. Speeches were delivered by G. Q. Cannon, Morris of

Left: SPIKE DRIVEN BY BRIGHAM YOUNG AT THE COMPLETION OF THE UTAH CENTRAL RAILWAY (OGDEN TO SALT LAKE CITY) ON 10 JANUARY 1870. COURTESY MUSEUM OF CHURCH HISTORY AND ART, SALT LAKE CITY.

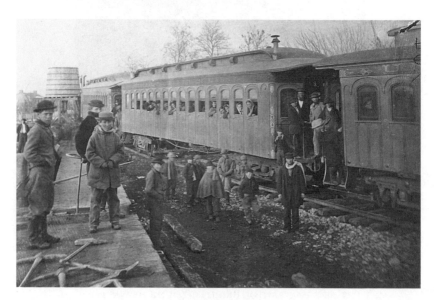

Above: THE FIRST TRAIN TO ARRIVE ON THE NEW UTAH CENTRAL RAILWAY ON 10 JANUARY 1870. COURTESY LDS CHURCH ARCHIVES, SALT LAKE CITY.

Right: "The Prest. and directors of Zion's Co-operative Mercantile Institution met at the Historian's office—Prest. Young presiding. The Directors instructed the Committee on appraisals to get up signs to be put over the Stores, the propriety of putting 'Holiness to the Lord' over the Stores on the sign boards was discussed. The Prest. offered to get up a sign for Eldredge and Clawson, which would serve as a pattern."[18] ZCMI sign, Charles W. Carter, about 1869. Courtesy LDS Church Archives, Salt Lake City.

UPRR & others. 36 guns were fired one for each mile of the road. In the evening we attended a great ball at the theater there was a pleasant atmosphere. Citizens of the city, Camp Douglas, our children saw the trains & locomotives for the first time."[19]

While this was a time of rejoicing, Brigham was also dealing with the new "movement," a break-off group seeking to re-define the mission of the kingdom. For Brigham, it was an additional heart-break because some of his close friends and associates joined the group, including former Apostle Amasa Lyman. Brigham noted in a letter to Albert Carrington that "It is truly astonishing how men will suffer themselves to be blinded by the spirit of darkness, totally regardless of every principle of right, old associations, testimonies, & intimate acquaintance with the truth, but so it is with many, the cares of

Above: First Presidency and Quorum of Twelve. This may be the first photograph ever taken of the entire First Presidency and the Quorum of the Twelve Apostles together, possibly by Charles R. Savage on 9 October 1868. Left to right: Orson Hyde, Orson Pratt, John Taylor, Wilford Woodruff, George A. Smith, Ezra T. Benson, Charles C. Rich, Brigham Young, Lorenzo Snow, Daniel H. Wells, Erastus Snow, Franklin D. Richards, George Q. Cannon, Brigham Young, Jr., and Joseph F. Smith. Courtesy Utah State Historical Society, Salt Lake City.

the world choke the good seed, & they are blinded & led captive to the will of the devil."[20]

In 1871 Brigham reached a milestone, his seventieth birthday. He was greeted by many guests. John Taylor spoke for the Quorum of the Twelve when they met briefly with him in the President's office on 1 June:

"Brother Brigham:

"We a few of the Twelve, who are now in the city, have called upon you to congratulate you upon this the Seventieth Anniversary of your Birthday. We are happy to find you in the enjoyment of good health, and that your bodily strength and general appearance indicate such remarkable preservation after an earthly sojourn of seventy years. We rejoice that through the blessings of Israel's God, you have been able to lead forth His people from the lands of the far-off East to these beautiful valleys of the mountains, which, under your counsel aided by the Spirit of our Heavenly Father, have spread and expanded to their present magnificent proportions.

"We look upon you, under the direction of Almighty God, as our Leader in the dictation of His Church and Kingdom in this land, and through the world; and as we have enjoyed your communion, counsel and fellowship for so many years past, we sincerely hope that your life may be prolonged to you for many years to come, and that we may have the pleasure of

Above: ILLUSTRATION FROM THE 25 NOVEMBER 1871 ISSUE OF THE *HARPER'S WEEKLY.* COURTESY GARY L. AND CAROL L. BUNKER, OREM, UTAH.

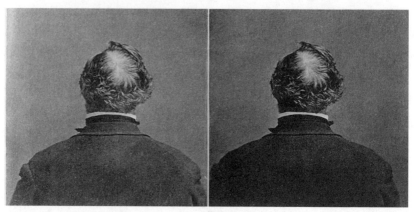

Above: BRIGHAM YOUNG, BY CHARLES R. SAVAGE, CA. 1871. COURTESY LDS CHURCH ARCHIVES, SALT LAKE CITY.

your associations in this world, and then be eternally united in the Celestial Kingdom of our God."[21]

While Elder Taylor was speaking, a reporter noted, "The emotion of those present was so great, that there was scarcely a dry eye in the room."[22]

As anti-polygamy pressures mounted, Brigham was arrested on a charge of "lascivious cohabitation." Shortly after his arrest, he found himself again making headline news throughout the nation. The 11 November 1871 issue of the *Leslie's Weekly* depicted Brigham, with a huge family, meeting U.S. President

Above: BRIGHAM YOUNG, BY CHARLES R. SAVAGE,
1 JUNE 1871. COURTESY LDS CHURCH ARCHIVES,
SALT LAKE CITY.

Grant. Under the title "The Mormon Problem Solved,"
Brigham Young asks Grant: "I must submit to your laws—but
what shall I do with all these?" President Grant replies: "Do as
I do—give them offices."

In April 1872 the U.S. Supreme Court nullified the actions
of Utah Territory Supreme Court Justice James B. McKean.
Soon thereafter Brigham was released after some 120 days
under guard. He appeared before the Saints on 28 April.

Above: CHARLES W. CARTER'S PHOTOGRAPH OF BRIGHAM YOUNG'S CARRIAGE, POSSIBLY ON 9 OCTOBER 1871. CHIEF JUSTICE McKEAN SENT U.S. MARSHAL PATRICK TO ARREST BRIGHAM YOUNG AT HIS HOME ON 2 OCTOBER. ON THE 9TH HE APPEARED IN COURT (HELD ON THE 2ND FLOOR OF A LIVERY STABLE OWNED BY FAUST AND HOUTZ, LOCATED ON SECOND SOUTH) BEFORE JUDGE McKEAN. COURTESY LDS CHURCH ARCHIVES, SALT LAKE CITY.

Below: U.S. SUPREME COURT, CA. 1876. COURTESY THE LIBRARY OF CONGRESS, WASHINGTON, D.C.

THE MORMON PROBLEM SOLVED.

Brigham—*"I must submit to your laws—but what shall I do with all these?"*
U. S. G.—*"Do as I do—give them offices."*

Above: Illustration from the 11 November 1871 issue of the *Leslie's Weekly.* Courtesy Gary L. and Carol B. Bunker, Orem, Utah.

"A word to the Latter-day Saints. Good morning. (Congregation responded, 'Good morning.') How do you do? (Congregation replied, 'Very well.') How is your faith this morning? ('Strong in the Lord,' was the response.) How do you think I look after my long confinement? (Congregation replied, 'First rate.'). . . . I will say a few words to you. The Gospel of the Son of God is most precious. My faith is not weakened in the Gospel in the least. I will answer a few of the questions that probably many would like to ask of me. Many would like to know how I have felt the past winter, and so much of the spring as is now past. I have enjoyed myself exceedingly well. I have been blessed with an opportunity to rest; and you who are acquainted with me and my public speaking can discern at once, if you listen closely to my voice, it is weak to what it used to be, and I required rest. I feel well in body and better in mind. I have no complaint to make, no fault to find, no reflections to cast, for all that has been done has been directed and overruled by the wisdom of Him who knows all things.

"As to my treatment through the winter, it has been very agreeable, very kind. My associate, my companion in tribula-

Left: BRIGHAM YOUNG BY AN UN-KNOWN ARTIST, CA. 1872. COURTESY MUSEUM OF CHURCH HISTORY AND ART, SALT LAKE CITY.

Above: Brigham Young, by Charles R. Savage, ca. 1872. Courtesy LDS Church Archives, Salt Lake City.

tion, I will say, has acted the gentleman as much as any man could. I have not one word, one lisp or beat of the heart to complain of him. He has been full of kindness, thoughtful, never intruding, always ready to hearken and, I think, in the future, will be perfectly willing to take the counsel of his prisoner. So much for Captain Isaac Evans. I will say this to you, ladies and gentlemen, you who profess to understand true etiquette, I have not seen a gentleman in my acquaintance that possesses more of the real spirit of gentility, caution and of true etiquette than Captain Evans."[23]

80   HARPER'S WEEKLY.   [JANUARY 27, 1872.

AMONG THE MORMONS.

POLYGAMY existed in Utah for nineteen years without any decided efforts having been made to put it down. Two years before BRIGHAM YOUNG first promulgated the "plurality" doctrine, based upon a supposed revelation from the prophet JOE SMITH, Utah had been declared a Territory of the States, but for a long while the government, with the exception of a great outcry by the Republican party in 1856, allowed BRIGHAM YOUNG and his apostles to do as they liked. Two years later there was a rumor that the Mormons were about to rise in revolt, and an expedition, under the command of Colonel JOHNSTON, afterward a general in the Confederate service, invaded Utah. He met, however, with such formidable resistance that he thought it best to temporize, and the only advantage for an ecclesiastical governor, the post having been formerly held by BRIGHAM YOUNG himself. Since then the government has been gradually gaining power and authority in Mormondom, but made no decisive attempt to put down polygamy until a short time ago, when Judge M'KEAN, an energetic reformer, declared his intention of indicting all polygamists, and arrested BRIGHAM YOUNG, and several of the leading Mormons. One of them—HAWKINS—has been tried, and sentenced to $500 fine and three years' imprisonment, the *minimum* punishment allowable by law.

To take a short retrospect of Mormon history. After trying to settle in Missouri, JOE SMITH emigrated with his followers to Illinois, where they were at first hospitably received. Here SMITH became powerful, was created a lieutenant-general of Mormon militia, and actually announced himself as a candidate for the Presidency of the United States. Jealousies between Mormons and Gentiles, however, arose. SMITH was frequently arrested, and one day a body of men broke into his prison at Carthage and murdered him. BRIGHAM YOUNG succeeded him as chief of the sect, and it was under his auspices that the emigration into Utah, then a Mexican wilderness, peopled only by Indians, was undertaken and accomplished. Arrived at Great Salt Lake, the Saints speedily set to work, and in a very short space of time the desert was transformed into a highly cultivated and productive country. The Indians were conciliated with kind usage and presents, and left the invaders unmolested, and where their wigwams alone had flourished a splendid and populous city speedily sprang up, BRIGHAM YOUNG took especial care with the building of the town, and ordained that the streets should be miles wide. He also paid great attention to sanitary precautions, whence Salt Lake City is universally acknowledged to be one of the most healthy residences on record. Viewed from the heights above, the town ap-

pears a little paradise, so refreshing does this oasis of civilization seem in contrast to the surrounding desert. It does not, however, appear to such an advantage when entered by the railway—that great reformer, to whose advance the Mormons owe their present misfortunes. Had it, indeed, not been for the "iron horse," and the important mineral discoveries lately made in the neighborhood—discoveries which have brought flocks of envious Gentiles to the Territory—BRIGHAM YOUNG might still have been all-powerful there instead of being a fugitive from justice, doubly accused of immorality and murder. Nor direct murder, be it understood, but murder through his orders. It appears that the Mormons had a disagreeable habit of getting rid of an obnoxious opponent by having him murdered, and that a special band of executioners, called "Destroying Angels" or "Danites," was maintained for that purpose, under the command of a man named HICKMAN. Several mysterious murders of Gentiles have been set down to this agency, and HICKMAN, who has been caught by the United States government, is said to have made revela-

tions inculpating BRIGHAM YOUNG, DANIEL H. WELLS, and several other prominent Mormons, for whom, accordingly, warrants of arrest have been issued.

To return to Salt Lake City. Besides making the streets wide, YOUNG planted trees at the side, and surrounded the houses with gardens, an acre and a quarter being allowed for each house and grounds. The great thoroughfare is "Main Street," where not only the principal hotels, banks, and stores are situated, but also the residences of BRIGHAM YOUNG and DANIEL H. WELLS. These are represented in our illustration, as well as the views north and west looking from the street. In spite of the trim appearance of the neat houses and carefully cultivated gardens, there is one great drawback—the street is entirely unpaved, and, there being no gas-works, wholly unlighted at night. One great characteristic of American cities is also absent: not a single drinking-shop is to be seen, no wines and spirits are prohibited, and in the entire city there are only two spirit bars, which are wholly frequented by thirsty Gentiles.

BRIGHAM YOUNG's house, beyond being somewhat larger, is little different from the other buildings. It is painted white, with green Venetians, while a smaller and almost detached building by the side, erected in Gothic style, serves for the residence of his sixteen wives. The Tabernacle forms the subject of another illustration. This (of the interior of which we gave an engraving some weeks ago) is only a temporary place of worship until the great Temple shall be finished. A huge, ugly, oval-shaped building, the Tabernacle is capable of containing an enormous concourse of people; and at a recent conference no less than 10,000 persons assembled there.

Rich in all agricultural produce, and in all the necessaries of life, the Mormons possess but very little money. Payment there is generally made in kind—*i. e.*, suppose A let a grocer indebted to B for chimney-sweeping, he pays him in an order for the amount in goods on his store. Should B not want the groceries, he pays the order away to C for so many loaves of bread. Thus, as there is very little trade with the Gentile world, there is no opportunity for the Mormons to accumulate money, and this he doubtless the secret of their great industry. Even here, however, the railway has wrought a change, and one of the reasons which Mormonism's the appearance of pretty women at the car window, while stopping at a station, offering pairs of handsomely braided gloves for sale.

The Saints are taking their misfortunes with singular quietude. At first the young men talked of resistance, but even the trial and condemnation of HAWKINS roused them no further, and it is now little likely that any armed opposition will be made to the proceedings of the United States authorities. BRIGHAM YOUNG has sur-

BRIGHAM YOUNG.

DANIEL H. WELLS.

AMONG THE MORMONS.

GEORGE A. SMITH.

Left: THE *HARPER'S WEEKLY* OF 27 JANUARY
1872 REPRODUCED A BEAUTIFUL SKETCH OF
BRIGHAM YOUNG. THE THREE-PAGE ARTICLE
INCLUDED VIEWS OF MAIN STREET (LOOKING
NORTH), MAIN STREET (LOOKING WEST); THE
RESIDENCES OF BRIGHAM YOUNG AND DANIEL
H. WELLS; THE TABERNACLE; AND ADDITIONAL
PORTRAITS OF DANIEL H. WELLS AND GEORGE
A. SMITH, BOTH COUNSELORS TO BRIGHAM
YOUNG IN THE FIRST PRESIDENCY AT THE
TIME. COURTESY R. Q. AND SUSAN SHUPE,
SAN JUAN CAPISTRANO, CALIFORNIA.

Below: PUBLISHED IN 1872 IN PHILADELPHIA BY WILLIAM FLINT & CO.,
THIS WOOD ENGRAVING IS TITLED "BRIGHAM YOUNG, HEAD OF THE MOR-
MON CHURCH, AND A PORTION OF HIS WIVES AND CHILDREN". COURTESY
GARY L. AND CAROL B. BUNKER, OREM, UTAH.

Brigham Young,
HEAD OF THE MORMON CHURCH, AND A PORTION OF HIS WIVES AND CHILDREN.

Ld. ILLUSTRATION FROM THE 16 APRIL 1873 ISSUE OF THE *DAILY GRAPHIC.* COURTESY GARY L. AND CAROL B. BUNKER, OREM, UTAH.

The *Daily Graphic* introduced their readers to Brigham, depicting him as Moses in the 16 April 1873 issue. The positive article stated:

"Our ILLUSTRATION. Away from the reach of locomotive and telegraph, 'The Mormon Moses' takes his pilgrimage to Arizona, to turn the wilderness into a garden and convert the Apaches to his faith. The civilization he created in Utah was peculiar, but it taught sobriety, industry, and just dealing. Its cause was polygamy, and its successor, while losing none of the old Mormon virtues, should add social purity as proof of its superiority. Brigham Young tells his own story: 'For over forty years I have served my people, laboring incessantly, and am now nearly seventy-two years of age and I need relaxation.' A farm laborer at thirty, he has stamped his name upon the age as one of its executive chiefs. The record of his forty years of labor entitles him to a place in the group of GRAPHIC Statues. A correct portrait of Brigham Young with a sketch of his life, and a picture of the Mormon Tabernacle at Salt Lake City, are given on the fourth page. The scene in the Tabernacle is taken on occasion of the recent semi-annual conference of the Saints, when the Mormon Prophet resigned his position as director of the business interests of his people."[24]

During November 1873 Brigham prepared instructions regarding his funeral and burial. This "Last Will and Testament" was followed upon his death in August 1877.

"I, Brigham Young, wish my funeral services to be conducted in the following manner:

"When I breathe my last I wish my friends to put my body in as clean and wholesome state as can conveniently be done, and preserve the same for one, two, three or four days, or as long as my body can be preserved in a good condition. I want my coffin made of plump 1 1/4 inch boards, not scrimped in length, but two inches longer than I would measure, and from

Right: BRIGHAM YOUNG, BY DAN WEGGLAND, 1873. COURTESY MUSEUM OF CHURCH HISTORY AND ART, SALT LAKE CITY.

two to three inches wider than is commonly made for a person of my breadth and size, and deep enough to place me on a little comfortable cotton bed, with a good suitable pillow for size and quality; my body dressed in my temple clothing, and laid nicely into my coffin, and the coffin to have the appearance that if I wanted to turn a little to the right or to the left, I should have plenty of room to do so. The lid can be made crowning.

"At my interment I wish all of my family present that can be conveniently, and the male members wear no crepe on their hats or on their coats; the females to buy no black bonnets, nor black dresses, nor black veils; but if they have them they are at liberty to wear them. The services may be permitted, as singing and a prayer offered, and if any of my friends wish to say a few words, and really desire, do so; and when they have closed their services, take my remains on a bier, and repair to the little burying ground, which I have reserved on my lot east of the White House on the hill, and in the southeast corner of this lot, have a vault built of mason work large enough to receive my coffin, and that may be placed in a box, if they choose, made of the same material as the coffin—redwood. Then place flat rocks over the vault sufficiently large to cover it, that the earth may be placed over it—nice, fine, dry earth—to cover it until the walls of the little cemetery are reared, which will leave me in the southwest corner. This vault ought to be roofed over with some kind of temporary roof. There let my earthly house or tabernacle rest in peace, and have a good sleep, until the morning of the first resurrection; no crying or mourning with anyone as I have done my work faithfully and in good faith.

"I wish this to be read at the funeral, providing that if I should die anywhere in the mountains, I desire the above directions respecting my place of burial to be observed; but if I should live to go back with the Church to Jackson County, I wish to be buried there. Brigham Young, President of the Church of Jesus Christ of Latter-day Saints, Sunday, November 9th, 1873, Salt Lake City, Utah."[25]

Right: BRIGHAM YOUNG, BY
SAMUEL JEPPERSON, 1875.
UTAH COUNTY ARTIST AND
MUSICIAN SAMUEL HANS
JEPPERSON WENT TO ST.
GEORGE IN OCTOBER 1874
TO ASSIST IN THE COMPLE-
TION OF THE TEMPLE BEING
REARED THERE. BRIGHAM
ARRIVED IN THE MORMON
SETTLEMENT ON 11 NOVEM-
BER 1874 AND STAYED IN
SOUTHERN UTAH UNTIL 10
FEBRUARY 1875. SOME TIME
DURING THE WINTER SEASON
JEPPERSON PICKED UP A
PIECE OF WOOD DISCARDED
BY THE TEMPLE CARPENTERS
AND PAINTED THIS OIL
PORTRAIT OF BRIGHAM.
WHETHER OR NOT BRIGHAM
SAT FOR THE PORTRAIT CAN-
NOT BE DETERMINED. COUR-
TESY MUSEUM OF CHURCH
HISTORY AND ART, SALT
LAKE CITY.

In 1875 Brigham confronted the death of long-time friend and counselor, George A. Smith, his eldest son, Joseph A. Young, and his wife Emmeline Free Young; visited the President of the United States; was arrested for contempt of court; and visited Baron Lionel de Rothschild.

George Q. Cannon wrote to Brigham's long-time non-Mormon friend Thomas L. Kane a short letter updating him on happenings in Utah. Elder Cannon included a personal reflection regarding Brigham: "Our friend has had a series of afflictions to bear since this year [1875] opened which would be

Left BRIGHAM YOUNG, BY FOX AND SYMONS, CA. 1875. COURTESY SPECIAL
COLLECTIONS, MERRILL LIBRARY, UTAH STATE UNIVERSITY, LOGAN, UTAH.

very trying [to] an ordinary man; but which he has borne with
exemplary patience, meekness, and equinimity. His daughter
Alice, his wife Emeline, his son Joseph A. and his trusted friend
and counselor George A. Smith, have all gone. Probably not
more than two events of his life ever afflicted him so deeply as
did the sudden departure of Joseph A. . . . One might imagine
[that] these events, with the other annoyances to which he has
been subjected of late, would way him down. . . . I am happy in
being able to say to you that he is as cheerful and courageous as
ever. Even when recently suffering from the disease which at-
tacked him in the fall of 1874, he was buoyant and lively. He
never seems to me, like an old man, or I would call him a grand
old man. At no time in his life did he ever seem to me to be a
more resolute, [commendable] soldier of righteousness than at
the present period. The Lord has endowed him with extraordinary strength and nerve. Having just been released from confinement when I left he was able to take his accustomed exercise and his health was improving."26

NOTES

1. In Richard O. Cowan, *Temples to Dot the Earth* (Salt Lake City:
Bookcraft, 1989), 66.

2. *Gleason's Pictorial Drawing-Room Companion* (3 January 1854),
345.

3. *Journal of Discourses* 4:112–13.

4. T. B. H. Stenhouse, *The Rocky Mountain Saints: A Full and Complete History of the Mormons* (New York: D. Appleton and Company,
1873), 539.

5. *Deseret News Weekly* 6 (10 December 1856): 320.

6. *Journal of Discourses* 5:77.

7. "Patriarchal Blessing, given G. S. L. Dec. 25, 1857 by John Young upon the head of Brigham Young," Brigham Young Papers, LDS Church Archives, Salt Lake City (hereafter cited as LDSCA).

8. "Blessing, 3 March 1859," Brigham Young Papers, LDSCA.

9. "General Church Minutes," 24 April 1859, LDSCA.

10. *Journal of Discourses* 8:8.

11. "Ordination Blessing, August 25, 1860, George Q. Cannon," Brigham Young Papers, LDSCA.

12. Historian's Office Journal, 28 April 1862, LDSCA.

13. Andrew Karl Larson, *Erastus Snow: The Life of a Missionary and Pioneer for the Early Mormon Church* (Salt Lake City: University of Utah Press, 1971), 601.

14. A. J. Allen Diary, 9–10 May 1863, Special Collections, Harold B. Lee Library, Brigham Young University, Provo, Utah.

15. Wilford Woodruff Journal, 1 July 1866; see Scott G. Kenney, ed., *Wilford Woodruff's Journal, 1833–1898*, 9 vols. (Midvale: Signature Books, 1983–85), 6:289–90.

16. Historian's Office Journal, 22 May 1868, LDSCA.

17. Brigham Young to Elder Brigham Young, Jr., 11 November 1869; Brigham Young Papers, LDSCA.

18. Historian's Office Journal, 29 October 1868.

19. Charles R. Savage Diary, 10 January 1870, Special Collections, Harold B. Lee Library, Brigham Young University, Provo, Utah.

20. Brigham Young to President A. Carrington, 2 February 1870, Brigham Young Papers, LDSCA.

21. Journal History, 1 June 1871, LDSCA.

22. Ibid.

23. *Journal of Discourses* 15:16–17.

24. *Daily Graphic*, 16 April 1873.

25. Brigham Young's "Last Will and Testament," 9 November 1873; as cited in Richard H. Cracroft and Neal E. Lambert, comp., *A Believing People: Literature of the Latter-day Saints* (Salt Lake City: Bookcraft, 1979), 72–73.

26. George Q. Cannon to Thomas L. Kane, 2 November 1875, typescript, Special Collections, Harold B. Lee Library, BYU.

ᘔ

Chapter 7
INTO THE SUNSET

While newspaper reports continually emphasized Brigham's health and youthful appearance, frequently underestimating his age by nearly a decade, he was often sick, and this debilitated or even incapacitated him for various lengths of time. Given the tremendous and heavy schedule he maintained through most of his life, it is a wonder that he survived some of the severe medical crises in his adult life.

During his last years Brigham was attended to by his nephew, Seymour B. Young, who was among the first Latter-day Saints sent East to medical school. During the final years President Young suffered from bouts with rheumatism and with urological difficulties. He continued to maintain a heavy work and travel schedule, which often wore him down. "Pres. Young is quite unwell again having worked himself clear down," his doctor noted in April 1875.[1]

In 1876 Brigham spent a significant amount of time visiting the Saints, holding meetings, and traveling to St. George to oversee the completion of the temple there. He left Salt Lake City on 1 May and returned on 1 July 1876. Leaving

Above: Brigham Young, by Charles R. Savage, ca. 1876.
Courtesy LDS Church Archives, Salt Lake City.

again for St. George on 1 November, he stayed through the winter to dedicate a portion of the St. George Temple in the spring of 1877.

While in St. George during the last two years of his life, as he did during all his visits, Brigham rekindled old friendships. Members of the Church who had known him for some time were appreciative of his attention. Charles L. Walker wrote in his diary in June 1876: "While I was on the stand He asked me to let him have an original copy of the Temple song which I

Above: ST. GEORGE TEMPLE UNDER CONSTRUCTION, MARCH 1876. COURTESY LDS CHURCH ARCHIVES, SALT LAKE CITY.

composed. After meeting I went home and got the song and took it to him. He treated me very kindly and asked me to sit beside him and take dinner with him. I spent the time very pleasantly and found him to be very polite, genial, and sociable, and I felt quite at home in Chatting over the work on the Temple, old times, and other general topics. In bidding him good bye He took my hand in both of his and said, God bless you Br Charley, and God has blessed you hasnt He? It seemed that in an instant all the blessings I had ever recei[v]ed were before Me. My emotion was too much to answer him and I chokeingly said, I have learned to trust in the Lord."[2]

It was during 1876 that the first full-length biography of Brigham appeared in New York City. The Historian's Office Journal reveals the open access that Edward Tullidge had during the previous year as he did research for his book. When published, the biography quickly went into second printing the following year.

Tullidge concluded his review of Brigham's life with this observation: "Brigham Young has led his people thirty-three years. Seldom does it fall to the lot of rulers to sway the scepter so long; still less seldom to keep up in their lives such an unwearied sensation. His name has now provoked and now charmed 'all the world.' A marvelous psychology has been in that name, to thus prevail. He has just completed his seventy-fifth year (June 1ˢᵗ, 1876). His will is still matchless; his mind still sound. View the man as we may, Brigham Young is an enduring name. The friction of centuries will not erase it."[3]

Within months of the general Church conference and dedication of the new temple in St. George, Brigham was again front-page news: "BRIGHAM YOUNG. On the 8ᵗʰ of April last Brigham Young was re-elected Prophet, Seer and Revelator, and President of the Church of Jesus Christ of Latter-Day Saints in all the world, at the Conference the Mormon Church held in the new Temple at St. George."[4]

Left. BRIGHAM YOUNG, BY CHARLES. R. SAVAGE, 1877. APPARENTLY THE LAST PHOTOGRAPH TAKEN OF BRIGHAM SOME TIME AFTER HIS ARRIVAL IN SALT LAKE CITY ON 29 APRIL 1877, HAVING SPENT THE WINTER IN ST. GEORGE. COURTESY SPECIAL COLLECTIONS-MANUSCRIPTS, J. WILLARD MARRIOTT LIBRARY, UNIVERSITY OF UTAH, SALT LAKE CITY.

Right: SALT LAKE TEMPLE
UNDER CONSTRUCTION, BY
CHARLES W. CARTER, CA.
1877. COURTESY LDS
CHURCH ARCHIVES, SALT
LAKE CITY.

Just before his birthday in June 1877, Brigham spoke to the Saints: "As to my health, I feel many times that I could not live an hour longer, but I mean to live just as long as I can. I know not how soon the messenger will call for me, but I calculate to die in harness."[5] Late in August 1877, however, Brigham's health quickly deteriorated.

He was not feeling well on the afternoon of the twenty-third, and by 11:00 P.M. he was "seized with violent vomiting, purging [i.e. diarrhea] and cramping" which lasted for the next six hours.[6]

The citizens of Utah learned of the illness Friday afternoon through a brief notice published in the *Deseret Evening News.*[7] Updated reports about Brigham's condition filled the telegraph line and was announced from pulpits, published in newspapers, and passed along by word of mouth. By Wednesday, 29 August, it was apparent that the end was near. Family, friends, and Church leaders gathered in the Lion House room where Brigham had been moved earlier, to watch him slip into eternity. While he remained in a coma most of the morning, he responded "in a clear and distinct voice, 'Amen'" after being administered to by several brethren.[8]

Above: LION HOUSE BEDROOM, CA. 1930, FROM SUSA YOUNG GATES'S *THE LIFE STORY OF BRIGHAM YOUNG*. THE BEDROOM WHERE BRIGHAM YOUNG DIED ON 29 AUGUST 1877, CONTAINING SOME OF THE ORIGINAL FURNISHINGS BELONGING TO HIS FAMILY.

The last words to fall from Brigham's lips were, "Joseph, Joseph, Joseph." Based on those words, Henry W. Naisbitt, assistant editor of the Church's newspaper in the British Isles, pub-lished a poem on 1 October 1877 entitled, "The Dying Prophet."[9]

"Joseph, Joseph, Joseph, Joseph;" softly murmured Zion's
chief,
As life's pulses weakened, ebbing, in the midst of loving grief;
Ah! The tale *that* tells is grander, than the epics, men have
moved,
For it speaks of recognition; Joseph—was the man he loved!

He, the dying, prostrate leader, grasped in death, the friend of
yore,

Come to give a welcome greeting, as he neared the other
    shore;
Faithful, steadfast, tried and trusted, well thy mission thou
    hast done,
Joseph meets thee, on the threshold, of the kingdom thou
    hast won!

True beside the great Ohio, true upon Missouri's plain,
True where Far West's prairies reaching, untouched by defec-
    tion's stain;
True where Mississippi's waters glassed the Temple's towering
    dome,
True when Carthage sent its victims to their desolated home!

True when fleeing from the hunters, as the antelope flees by;
True when camped 'mid death and sorrow, 'neath the silent
    winter sky;
True in all that wondrous passage,—pilgrimage to peace, from
    strife,
True in Utah's proud dominions, marked by thy devoted life!

This the mission Jesus gave thee, Joseph on thy shoulders laid,
When his great heart quivered—feeling, that his life would be
    betrayed;
So he passed in trust unshaken, as by revelation filled:
Joseph, Brigham, neither faltered, until death their efforts
    stilled.

And when murmuring softly—"Joseph," proudly thou
    could'st sink to rest,
On the outer verge of glory, frankly greet "The Prophet"
    blest!
Ah, that meeting! who can grasp it, realize the surging swell,
Of those hearts who proved through all things, that affec-
    tion—acts best tell?

Who would falter? Mark their leader, emulate his life, his
    death;

Welcome they shall have when passing, greeting friends with
    latest breath;
Jesus, Joseph; Joseph, Brigham, 'twas triumphant music there;
Angel bands for introduction, every faithful soul shall share![10]

Brigham's grandson Richard Young recorded his description of the fateful moment when Brigham slipped away: "He
sank from one stage of dissolution to another so easily and
rapidly that at one minute past Four he rendered up his spirit
and the person of Brigham Young, so long and favorably
known to his thousands of followers, as a great and good and
magnanimous man but to all the intelligent world as a practicer
of righteous precepts, lay lifeless & powerless among those who
were accustomed to call him father and friend, and to whom
they were wont to resort for spiritual and temporal adjuration.
It was gratifying to think that he departed comfortably and
placidly, evidently undisturbed by that pain which had been
racking his body during his illness. It was but a gasp or two—a
slight and almost imperceptible tremor—the rush of a thimble
of blood to his lips—when his pulse ceased to denote the vibra-
tion of his heart—his countenance assumed the blanched palor
of death, and all was quiet in the room save the sobs . . . of a
grieved and bereft family and friends."[11]

While the malady was unknown at the time, Brigham probably died of appendicitis, a clinical entity officially discovered in
1886.[12] On the following day the news of his passing spread
across the nation and throughout the world. The *San Francisco
Chronicle* noted: "The Mormon Prophet is dead. Brigham
yielded up his life yesterday at Salt Lake City, aged 76 years two
months and 29 days. It was a long, eventful, and a marvelous
life, considering the surrounding conditions of it. The rise of
Mohammed from poverty and obscurity to be the ruler of millions is an event without a parallel in history."[13]

Even the often hostile *Tribune* captured Brigham's spirit
when it reported: "At 4 o'clock precisely on yesterday afternoon Brigham Young, President of the Church of Jesus Christ

of Latter-day Saints, breathed his last at his residence, in this city. . . . He was in the main unconscious from yesterday until the time of his death, but during a brief interval, a few hours before dissolution, he recovered consciousness and spoke a few words to those around him. His vitality was wonderful, and he clung to life with a tenacity characteristic of the living Brigham Young. . . . And he who had attracted the attention of the world, hardly second in extent to any other ruler, quietly passed away from earth."[14]

Our last visual images of Brigham were made on the same day on which these obituaries appeared. George M. Ottinger came to the Lion House and made a plaster of paris cast of Brigham's right hand and a death mask. A clerk in the President's office noted: "A Plaster of Paris mold of his face and hands was taken this morning—countenance seems as though he was quietly sleeping."[15]

Below: BRIGHAM YOUNG'S DEATH MASK AND HAND CAST PREPARED BY GEORGE M. OTTINGER, 1 SEPTEMBER 1877. COURTESY MUSEUM OF CHURCH HISTORY AND ART, SALT LAKE CITY.

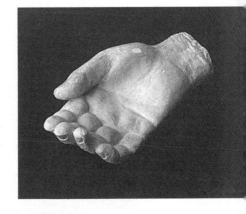

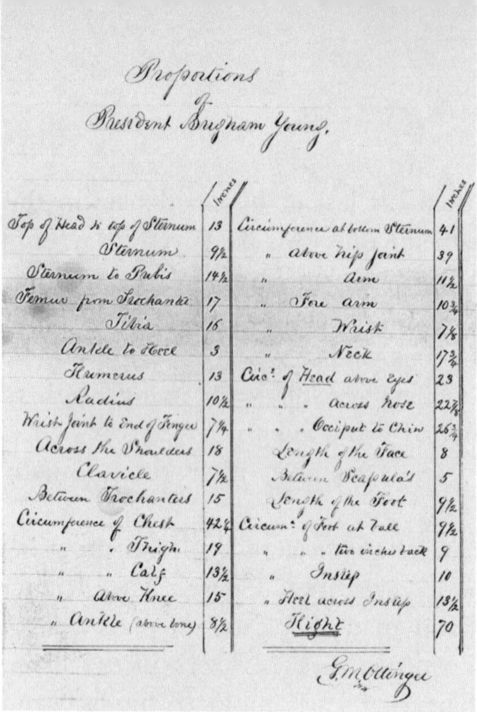

Proportions
of
President Brigham Young.

	Inches		Inches
Top of Head to top of Sternum	13	Circumference at bottom Sternum	41
Sternum	9½	" above hip joint	39
Sternum to Pubis	14½	" Arm	11½
Femur from Trochanta	17	" Fore arm	10¾
Tibia	16	" Wrist	7⅛
Ankle to Heel	3	" Neck	17¾
Humerus	13	Circ: of Head above eyes	23
Radius	10½	" " across nose	22⅞
Wrist joint to end of Finger	7¼	" " Occiput to Chin	26¾
Across the Shoulders	18	Length of the Face	8
Clavicle	7½	Between Scapula's	5
Between Trochanters	15	Length of the Foot	9½
Circumference of Chest	42½	Circum: of Foot at ball	9½
" " Thigh	19	" " " two inches back	9
" " Calf	13½	" Instep	10
" above Knee	15	" Heel across Instep	13½
" Ankle (above bone)	8½	Hight	70

G.M. Ottinger

Left: "PROPORTIONS OF PRESIDENT BRIGHAM YOUNG," CA. 1877. IT IS NOT CERTAIN WHEN GEORGE M. OTTINGER PREPARED THIS OUTLINE OF BRIGHAM YOUNG'S PROPORTIONS. POSSIBLY IT WAS AT THE TIME OF DEATH. COURTESY LDS CHURCH ARCHIVES, SALT LAKE CITY.

Below: TABERNACLE, BY CHARLES W. CARTER, 1877. COURTESY LDS CHURCH ARCHIVES, SALT LAKE CITY.

Right: WILD FLOWERS FROM BRIGHAM'S CASKET MADE INTO AN ARRANGEMENT BY HIS DAUGHTERS. COURTESY MUSEUM OF CHURCH HISTORY AND ART, SALT LAKE CITY.

Based on Brigham's own instructions the funeral was held on 2 September. Robert T. Burton noted in his journal: "Sunday, 2nd I came to the tabernacle at 8 a.m. and assisted during the day in arranging the Procession and other matters pertaining the funeral of the Prest. The procession formed at one thirty about 18000 people viewed the remains and more than this attended the funeral. All was very orderly."[16] Another observer, Mary Ann Burnham Freeze, wrote introspectively: "Sunday 2nd Attended Pres. Young's funeral, listened to some beautiful remarks, made by the twelve and some others, who spoke eulogistically of the deceased. Bro. Cannon said His the Pres. life seemed perfect to him. It was sad

Left: FUNERAL RIBBON, POSSIBLY PREPARED FOR THE FUNERAL, CA. 1877. COURTESY MUSEUM OF CHURCH HISTORY AND ART, SALT LAKE CITY.

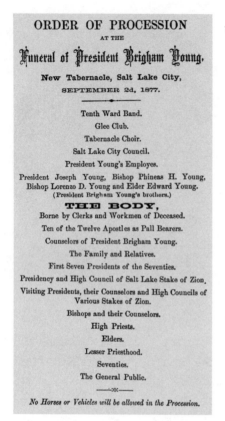

Left: PRINT "ORDER OF PROCES-SION" FOR FUNERAL. COURTESY UTAH STATE HISTORICAL SOCIETY, SALT LAKE CITY.

indeed to see the coffin borne towards its last resting place, by his four remaining brothers, I resolved that day that I would henceforth be more faithful in carrying out the consels of our beloved Prophet. I could see more plainly how faithfully he had laboured to perfect the Saints."[17]

John Farr recalled: "While the immense crowd lined the sidewalk but was kept back by ropes stretched along the line of shade trees, passing the Tithing Office [where the Joseph Smith Memorial Building now stands], entering the Eagle Gate, moving up the hill, entering the private cemetery of the deceased. At the grave side the family took its final view, after which the public had an opportunity of viewing the remains before it was lowered to its final resting place. The Glee Club sang, 'Oh My Father,' the dedicatory prayer by Wilford

Woodruff. This concluded the services and earthly career of . . .
one of the world's greatest characters."[18]

The *Deseret News* reported shortly after Brigham's burial:
"Large Rock—A large granite slab has been brought from the
Temple Quarry and is now on the Temple Block. It is ten feet
nine inches long, by six feet nine inches wide, and twenty
inches thick. It weights nine tons, one thousand five hundred
pounds. We under stand that, after being dressed, it is to be
placed over the vault containing the remains of the late President Brigham Young. After being placed in position it will be
covered with turf."[19]

During the following year the stone was ready to be placed
on the grave site: "Large Slab—This morning the large granite
slab to be placed over the tomb of the late President Brigham
Young, was conveyed from the Temple Block to the family
cemetery, for that purpose. Now that the stone is dressed it
measures 10 feet 10 inches long, 6 feet 7 inches wide, and 13
inches thick. It weights nearly seven tons."[20]

In 1884 the *Deseret Evening News* announced: "The private cemetery of the late President Brigham Young has recently been undergoing a series of improvements, which, though yet incomplete, have materially enhanced the appearance of the place. . . . The interior has been leveled and graded, that is, the northern half has, which was formerly partitioned off by a high stone wall. . . . The wall having been . . . removed, the north side will next be seeded, laid out and cultivated corresponding with the other. . . . The fence is a very handsome specimen of home casting. The front gates are centered with the monogram B.Y., and at the base of each post is a beehive, the emblem and synonym of Deseret. The pickets of the fence correspond with those around the President's grave, which remains the same as heretofore."[21]

Below: THE 3 SEPTEMBER 1877 ISSUE OF THE *MILLENNIAL STAR* CONTAINING AN OBITUARY BY HENRY W. NAISBITT.

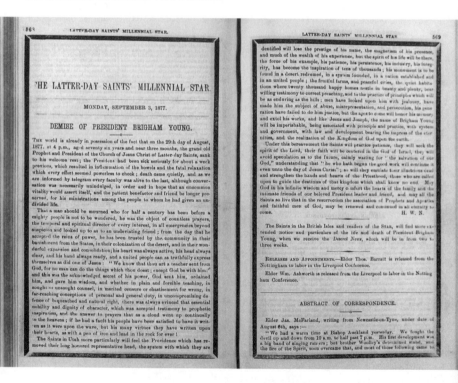

BRIGHAM YOUNG.

THE death of Brigham Young, on the 29th of August last, in his seventy-seventh year, will probably hasten the crisis toward which Mormon affairs have been working for some years. The Mormon system has owed its perpetuity and strength in the main to this man's extraordinary ability as a governor in matters civil and religious. In fact, from the time of his accession to the Presidency of the Mormon community, in 1847, to his death, he held the fortunes of his fellow religionaries in his hand, and in spite of the encroachments of other colonists and other religious societies, and notwithstanding the unfavorable attitude of the United States Government, he maintained the social and religious individuality of the Mormon community substantially unimpaired. He was a natural leader and organizer—a nation builder. Had he established his people in a country where they could have acquired the position of a separate, independent State, he would probably have founded a vigorous little nation. In his personal habits he was frugal and simple. He excelled as a judge of human nature and in the power of control. An unlearned man, yet he was able to build up a great, enterprising, and prosperous community, and to keep it always subordinate to his will. Take him all and all, Brigham Young was the most remarkable man of the century.

Left: THE *PHRENOLOGICAL JOURNAL* PUBLISHED A BRIEF OBITUARY IN THE OCTOBER 1877 ISSUE AND AN ARTICLE THAT INCLUDED A LINE DRAWING OF BRIGHAM YOUNG IN THE NOVEMBER 1877 ISSUE. COURTESY R. Q. AND SUSAN SHUPE, SAN JUAN CAPISTRANO, CALIFORNIA.

Overleaf: TWO PAGES FROM THE 15 SEPTEMBER 1877 ISSUE OF THE *FRANK LESLIE'S ILLUSTRATED NEWSPAPER.* COURTESY GARY L. AND CAROL B. BUNKER, OREM, UTAH.

FRANK LESLIE'S ILLUSTRATED NEWSPAPER

Entered according to the Act of Congress, in the year 1877, by Frank Leslie, in the Office of the Librarian of Congress at Washington.

No. 1,146—Vol. XLV.]   **NEW YORK, SEPTEMBER 15, 1877.**   [Price, 10 Cents. {$4.00 Yearly. In Weeks, $1.00.

THE LATE BRIGHAM YOUNG.

BRIGHAM YOUNG, Prophet, Seer and Revelator, and President of the Church of Jesus Christ of Latter-Day Saints in all the World, died at Salt Lake City, on the afternoon of Wednesday, August 29th. He was born at Whittingham, Vermont, June 1st, 1801. He joined the Mormons in 1832, at Kirtland, Ohio, and his energetic shrewdness soon secured for him an influential status. In 1835 he was one of the twelve apostles sent out to make converts. On the death of Joe Smith in 1844 he was chosen President and Prophet. After the disasters at Nauvoo, he, with a majority of the sect, abandoned that location early in 1846. He then announced that the Salt Lake Valley had been re-

vealed as the Promised Land, and founded Salt Lake City in July, 1847. In the Spring of 1849, immigration having greatly increased the Mormon ranks, a State was organized by the rulers, which they termed Deseret, but which Congress refused to admit as such into the Union, constituting in place thereof the Territory of Utah, of which, in 1850, Brigham Young was appointed United States Governor. Up to 1854 this state of things existed, but the Mormons subsequently defied the laws and officers of the Federal authority. In 1857 President Buchanan appointed Alfred Cumming Governor of Utah, and sent an army of 2,500 men to enforce his authority. In November, 1857, Governor Cumming proclaimed the Mormons as in a state of rebellion, but in 1858 a compromise was effected by which

the Federal authority was to be respected, and Brigham Young left in power as President and Ruler of the Mormon Church.

He was six feet high, and uncommonly compact and well-muscled. He measured forty-four inches around the chest, and such was his breadth in midperson that strangers who saw him for the first time, in his short, gray business-coat, imagined him a rather "stumpy" man, several inches shorter than he was. His head was of moderate size, with strong development of the basic and posterior regions of the cranium, and was by no means lacking in anterior breadth. His hair was chestnut if not colored, abundant in growth, and combed in a pedantic style into a foretop to the right side, with somewhat of the top of a rooster's comb. Brigham

Young had nineteen wives; fifteen of these were his own for time and eternity; the other four were proxy wives, being widows of Joseph Smith. The children of their union with Brigham are credited to Joseph Smith, and go to swell his kingdom. All plural wives are known by their maiden names, to distinguish one from the other. The following is a correct list of Brigham's wives, in the order of their marriage: Mary Ann Angel, Lucy Decker, Mrs. Augusta Cobb, Harriet Cook, Clara Decker, Emeline Free, Lucy Bigelow, Zina D. Huntington, Susan Snively, Margaret Pierce, Mrs. Twiss, Emily Partridge, Martha Boker, Eliza Burgess, Eliza R. Snow, Harriet Barney, Amelia Folsom, Mary Van Cott, and Ann Eliza Webb, the nineteenth and last.

(Continued on page 22.)

ACROSS THE CONTINENT.—THE FRANK LESLIE EXCURSION TO THE PACIFIC—A VISIT TO THE LATE PRESIDENT BRIGHAM YOUNG, IN SALT LAKE CITY.
FROM A SKETCH BY HARRY OGDEN.

1. The Old Residence. 2. The New Residence. 3. Mrs. Emmeline Young's House. 4. Mrs. Amelia Young's House. 5. Mrs. Cobb Young's House. 6. Social Hall. 7. Metropolitan Schoolhouse
SOME OF THE LATE BRIGHAM YOUNG'S RESIDENCES IN SALT LAKE CITY.

VIEW ON MAIN STREET, SALT LAKE CITY, IMMEDIATELY AFTER THE ANNOUNCEMENT OF BRIGHAM YOUNG'S DEATH, AUGUST 29TH.

UTAH.—THE DEATH OF BRIGHAM YOUNG, PROPHET, SEER AND REVELATOR, AND PRESIDENT OF THE CHURCH OF JESUS CHRIST OF LATTER-DAY SAINTS IN ALL THE WORLD.—SEE PAGE 17.

Brigham's death in 1877 brought him again into the public's eye.[22] Both LDS periodicals and magazines and non-LDS publications spent the next several weeks and months giving their audience a view of his life and labors. Some reports were kind and glowing; others harked back to the old stereotypes of former days.

By 1877 Frank Leslie was a very influential publisher with well over a dozen periodicals, of which the most important was *Frank Leslie's Illustrated Newspaper.* This paper sold as many as four hundred thousand copies an issue on occasions. Just weeks before Brigham died, Mr. and Mrs. Frank Leslie visited the aging prophet in Salt Lake City. They reported their visit in the 15 September 1877 issue of the paper.

According to the Leslies' account, Brigham asked them to "promise at least that you will print me as you have found me, and not as others have described me."[23]

NOTES

1. Seymour B. Young Diary, 18 April 1875, Utah State Historical Society.

2. Charles Lowell Walker Diary, 11 June 1876; see A. Karl Larson and Katharine Miles Larson, eds., *Diary of Charles Lowell Walker,* 2 vols. (Logan: Utah State University Press, 1990), 1:427.

3. Edward W. Tullidge, *Life of Brigham Young* (New York: n.p., 1876), 457–58.

4. *Frank Leslie's Illustrated Newspaper* (30 June 1877): 1.

5. *Journal of Discourses* 18:357.

6. Seymour B. Young Diary, 23 August 1877, Utah State Historical Society.

7. *Deseret Evening News,* 24 August 1877.

8. Ibid., 31 August 1877.

9. *Millennial Star* 39 (1 October 1877): 656.

10. Ibid.

11. Richard Young Diary, 29 August 1877, LDS Church Archives, Salt Lake City (hereafter cited as LDSCA).

12. See Lester E. Bush, Jr., "Brigham Young in Life and Death: A Medical Overview," *Journal of Mormon History* 5 (1978): 100.

13. *San Francisco Chronicle*, 30 August 1877.

14. [Salt Lake City] *Tribune*, 30 August 1877.

15. "1 September 1877," Brigham Young Papers, LDSCA.

16. Robert Taylor Burton Diary, 2 September 1877, LDSCA.

17. Mary Ann Burnham Freeze Diary, 2 September 1877, Special Collections, Harold B. Lee Library, BYU.

18. "An Account of the Funeral of President Brigham Young as Given by John Farr in a Letter to President George Albert Smith March 28, 1949," LDSCA.

19. *Deseret Evening News*, 17 September 1877.

20. Journal History, 21 March 1878, LDSCA.

21. *Deseret Evening News*, 6 August 1884.

22. See Gary L. Bunker and Davis Bitton, "The Death of Brigham Young: Occasion for Satire," *Utah Historical Quarterly* 54 (Fall 1986): 358–70.

23. Frank Leslie, *California: A Pleasure Trip from Gotham to the Golden Gate* (New York: G. W. Carleton and Company, 1877), 103.

CONCLUSION

Brigham knew, as well as anyone did, how intrusive journalists and writers could be, since he found himself time and time again the focus of critical reviews of almost everything he did, said, wrote, or tried to accomplish. On 10 April 1873 Brigham responded to an opportunity to answer a series of questions from the New York *Herald*. In concluding his reply, his optimism surfaced as he contemplated future generations: "My whole life is devoted to the Almighty's service, and while I regret that my mission is not better understood by the world, the time will come when I will be understood, and I leave to futurity the judgment of my labors and their result as they shall become manifest."[1]

In our day Elder Neal A. Maxwell has reflected: "Many think of President Brigham Young as primarily a great colonizer and governor, and excellent he was in those roles. But President Young, much more than being a colonizer and a governor, was a seer and a profound teacher of gospel doctrines and principles. The more one encounters his key teachings, the larger he looms."[2] Certainly Brigham is being evaluated more fairly today, and in some cases appreciated more than in the past.

Left. BRIGHAM
YOUNG, POSSIBLY
BY JOHN WILLARD
CLAWSON. COUR-
TESY MUSEUM OF
CHURCH HISTORY
AND ART, SALT
LAKE CITY.

While vilified repeatedly in the press during his life, Brigham nevertheless willingly met with almost all who came to Salt Lake City. Many came away from brief encounters with Brigham with a reverent respect if not downright admiration for him, his people, and what they had accomplished. What they subsequently wrote about these visits gives us a glimpse of Brother Brigham from a non-Mormon perspective. These recollections, the reminiscences and diary accounts of members of the Church, and Brigham's own words added to the visual images and help give us both a physical and a character reference point that makes Brigham real and personal. His comments were often candid, his pronouncements insightful, his spirituality deep, and his humor delightful. Many observed the depth of the man's intellect and sincerity in his eyes, his determination in his chin, and his love for the Saints in his words of exhortation, counsel, and direction.

When asked why we are sometimes left alone and often sad, Brigham told the small gathering at the President's office in January 1857: "Man is destined to be a God and has to act as an independent being—and is left without aid to see what he will do, whether he will be for God and to practice him to depend on his own resources, and try his independency—*to be righteous in the dark*—to be the friend of God and do the best I can when left to myself—act on my agency as the independent Gods, and show our capacity."[3]

As the ancient Apostle Paul reflected, "For now we see through a glass, darkly; but then face to face; now I know in part; but then shall I know even as also I am known,"[4] so Brigham's image is only imperfectly reflected in the mirrors of the black ink of the primary sources left behind and the flat photographic record and portrait paintings of him that have survived the ravages of time. In contrast, the day will come when Brigham will be seen and known as the Lord knows him full and infinitely now. Then we too will see Brigham as he really was—"righteous in the dark."

NOTES

1. *Millennial Star* 35 (10 April 1873): 287.
2. Neal A. Maxwell, "Brigham Young," in *Heroes of the Restoration* (Salt Lake City: Bookcraft, 1997), 219.
3. President's Office Journal, 28 January 1857, Brigham Young Papers, LDS Church Archives, Salt Lake City; emphasis added.
4. 1 Corinthians 13:12.

INDEX